Surviving the Scarlet Letter

Freedom from Shame

Karen Melville Thacker

WestBow
PRESS
A DIVISION OF THOMAS NELSON

WestBow Press books may be ordered through booksellers or by contacting:

WestBow Press
A Division of Thomas Nelson
1663 Liberty Drive
Bloomington, IN 47403
www.westbowpress.com
1-(866) 928-1240

ISBN: 978-1-4497-3735-1 (sc)
ISBN: 978-1-4497-3736-8 (hc)
ISBN: 978-1-4497-3737-5 (e)

Library of Congress Control Number: 2012900973

Printed in the United States of America

WestBow Press rev. date: 4/9/2012

For my husband: without your support and encouragement this book would be buried in an unorganized computer file and forgotten.

And for my children: by no choice of your own, you travelled this journey with me and still love me.

Contents

Introduction

WHAT IS THE SCARLET LETTER, YOU may ask? I got the name from the novel, *The Scarlet Letter,* which was written by Nathaniel Hawthorne and published in 1850. The story unfolds the details of an affair between a young married woman, Hester Prynne, and her pastor. The affair produces a child and a permanent change of course for Hester. Hester maintains silence and never reveals the identity of her partner in crime even though he is the very one to dole out her punishment. Unable to sentence her to death, he instead assigns her to a lifetime of bearing a scarlet A on her chest. It is the mark of her adultery, the stain of shame and scorn from anyone she encounters. Hester lives alone with her daughter, Pearl and spends years of her life in isolation from the usual community of women. It is in this isolation that she grows to accept her position and develops a strong character and understanding of humanity.

I first read *The Scarlet Letter* in my high school American Literature class. While I was engaged in my own affair, I reread the novel, gaining insight I had never noticed before. I personally experienced the saying, "It takes one to know one." *Surviving the Scarlet Letter* is about my journey. Although the debris left floating in my wake as a result of my own scarlet letter is painful to gaze upon, a few new shoots of positive growth have emerged. I have a greater understanding of not only myself but also God's grace, mercy, and unending forgiveness. I have developed empathy for all of us as we stumble around in our humanity and suffer the consequences of things we have shattered to pieces. This book is born out of my desire to encourage others to grow through their own experiences or walk alongside someone they care about who is perhaps in the process of making a mess of things.

For those who believe in positive and negative forces, you will understand me when I say that many times I believed Satan when he infused me with the belief that I am good for nothing. I thought of myself as being much like Hester Prynne, destined to a life of solitude and shame. Over time, it seems God has shown me that He wants more from me than that. I believe He wants me to break my silence, to step out and publicly disclose my experience, and to let others know that they are not alone. I have written this to let them know that affairs, whether emotional or physical, are dangerous but not a death sentence. For all of us who have done anything we regret and keep in hiding, my intent is to speak hope and encouragement and to remind us that God is the God of many chances. As long as He gives us breath, He has a purpose for our lives, and it is our job to live that out, not to cower in shame.

No more hiding!

Acknowledgements

URING THE FALL OF 2010 I sat on my nearly finished book. I didn't know what to do with it. Should I continue? Should I pursue getting it published? Is it even worth the time? A friend told me about an acquaintance who was involved in the writing world and gave me her name. I called Kirsten Otey and presented my dilemma to her. She said she'd take a look at it and let me know her thoughts. Much to my surprise she actually liked it! Her encouragement to continue with this project is part of the reason it has gotten this far. Thank you, Kirsten for giving me honest feedback and editing the first three chapters. You stretched me as a writer and breathed life into the possibilities of how this book might be used to encourage others.

Wendy Redal, a professional journalist and friend, also played a role in getting this book off the ground. I presented her with a very raw sketch of what I wanted to accomplish by writing this book. At the time I had 20 pages written. She encouraged me to create a skeleton of what I wanted to write. That skeleton has emerged into a complete body. I'm thankful to you, Wendy for taking the time to give me guidance. More importantly, I'm thankful for your kindness and understanding. You were one of the few who never abandoned me.

There are many people at Westbow Press who helped in the publishing process: David Roushia, Dustin Gearlds, Sam Fitzgerald, Angela McKellip, as well as the editing, design, and production teams. To all of you, thank you for your time, talent, patience, guidance, and encouragement. This book is the work of many hands, not just mine and I am grateful for your knowledge, wisdom, and insight.

There are some hard things written in this book, especially about my parents. It's important to me that you are aware that despite the not so great things they've done, my parents are amazing, generous, salt of the earth people. Like all of us, they have both fabulous and hurtful qualities. My family, while dysfunctional at times, is the best! I love when we are all together. The older we get the more real we are as our facades are peeling away along with our youthful glow. From my parents to my grandchildren, I love you all and am incredibly thankful that I get to call you family!

My journey was at times very lonely. I lost a lot of friends in the process, but I also made a few. Margi, Nan, Nikki, Patty, Michelle, Deirdre, Rita and Mary thank you for not deserting me during the least pleasant part of my history. Your presence in my life provided comfort at a time when I had none.

Finally, I want to acknowledge my accountability partner and friend, Karen. God has used you in profound ways throughout my journey. Thank you for making a very difficult choice to be my friend when you had plenty of opportunity to go a different direction. It does not usually bode well for the one who chooses the villain…I hope that your experience with me has been an anomaly! Thank you for keeping truth in front of me and reminding me of God's love for me. I appreciate your vulnerability and the kind of friendship that is two-way...we are both works in progress!

And always, thank you to my Father. Without Your grace, mercy and forgiveness, I would not have written about my journey from a position of hope!

I was shown mercy so that Jesus' immense
patience could be displayed.
I Timothy 1:16

Timeline

1994 Summer ~ My husband, John and I join a group of people from our church to start a non-denominational, seeker-friendly church.

1996 Summer ~ Ethan (not his real name) is hired as the new lead pastor of our church and we meet for the first time. I become the volunteer leader of the drama team.

1997 Fall ~ A team of six people from our church, including Ethan and me, travel to a conference together. I experience an intense connection with Ethan, get home, box it away, and forget about it.

2001 August ~ Ethan offers me a job to join the church staff.

2001 December ~ Ethan reveals his attraction to me and I acknowledge mine to him. We continue to work together.

2003 Summer ~ Ethan and I cross the physical boundary.

2003 Fall ~ My husband reads my journal after suspecting I was having an affair with Ethan, I claim it was in my head and later that it was only an emotional affair; I quit my job. John and I unsuccessfully try couples' counseling.

2004 May ~ Church elders ask us to leave the church.

2004 Summer ~ I tell my parents about my affair. I have the longest, yet still unsuccessful attempt at ending my relationship with Ethan.

2005 January ~ John gives me an ultimatum: our marriage or leave. I choose to leave and make plans to do so after our daughter's upcoming hospitalization.

2005 February ~ Anna is at Children's Hospital. I start seeing a Shadow Work coach. After Anna returns home, I move in with friends.

2005 April ~ I move into a studio apartment.

2005 Spring/Summer ~ Ethan is let go from the church after refusing to stop seeing me. He moves out of his house.

2005 July ~ I start a graduate program for counseling.

2005 Fall ~ I rent a house.

2005 December ~ My divorce is final.

2007 June ~ I graduate with a Master's degree in Counseling.

2007 August ~ I open my private practice.

2007 Late Fall ~ Ethan's divorce is final.

2008 Early February ~ My relationship with Ethan ends. I start seeing a counselor.

2008 June ~ I meet David.

2008 July ~ I attend the Cloud and Townsend Ultimate Leadership Intensive.

2008 September ~ Ethan calls and wants to reconnect with me. Permanent freedom from my relationship with Ethan.

2008 – Present ~ I am committed to experiencing freedom from my scarlet letter!

Chapter 1

A Dangerous Slide

IT WAS FRIDAY, DECEMBER 7, 2001. I had been working as the programming coordinator for a large and thriving nondenominational church for five months. This was my first job outside the home after spending the previous ten years raising my three children, who were ten, eight and five at the time. I wasn't entirely qualified for the role, but I was determined to master the learning curve. The position involved spending hours with the pastor and a team of sound, lighting, media, and music performance leads to produce a well-orchestrated church service designed to capture the attention of the audience in a manner similar to a rock concert. It was an exciting work environment. The technical success or failure of any given service fell on my shoulders, and I welcomed the challenge.

On this fateful December night, after the staff had gone home, my boss called me into his office to talk. Let's call him Ethan. We'd met five years earlier at a picnic welcoming him as our new pastor.

Prior to Ethan's arrival, our church had been led by a man who, while qualified to be a pastor, was operating a lucrative business and leading the church in his spare time. He knew the church needed a more available pastor to move it forward, and Ethan was hired. I didn't think much of him at that first meeting, other than to note his sense of humor and casual appearance. I had just had my third child two weeks prior to the picnic and was relishing the fact that for the first time in several years, I wasn't involved in any aspect of the church. I'd held volunteer positions in the drama ministry and the children's ministry. I had also served as the only female member of the executive leadership of the church. I was burned out and had been disappointed with the direction of the part-time pastor's teaching. In fact, my husband and I had been looking for a new church just prior to Ethan's arrival.

Ethan's teaching was dynamic and biblically sound. After he joined the staff, we decided to stay. We invited Ethan and his wife over for lunch one Sunday to welcome them and get acquainted. Ethan was charismatic, his wife more reserved. They seemed to have the common connection found in opposites. I enjoyed spending time with them, getting to know them. Over the years, Ethan's wife and I became friends. We shared meals together, offered parenting advice, and when their second child was born, we watched their son.

Over time, as Ethan grew more comfortable in our community, his sense of humor began to emerge. It became apparent that he was drenched in vitality, and people swarmed around him like bees on cherry blossoms, wanting not only to be around him but also to join him in his endeavors. To both my surprise and delight, Ethan asked if he and I could meet to talk about ways I could volunteer again with the church. He had been told about my prior involvement in the church and wanted to know if I would take on the task of leading the drama ministry. I said yes.

In October of 1997, a group from our church traveled to Chicago for a conference. My husband stayed behind and Ethan's wife helped watch our kids while he was at work. Six people piled into my van for the eighteen-hour drive. Ethan and I ended up sitting together. We spent hours laughing and talking in the back of the van. When it was our turn to share the driving responsibilities during the middle of the night shift, Ethan drove. We talked the entire time. For several hours, we conversed about life and our worldviews. Ethan had the ability to draw me out, and the conversation flowed seamlessly.

Something happened during that drive. Through the sharing, the fun, and the newness of a friendship that was forming, a part of me that had been dormant began to awaken. Without being fully cognizant of what was happening, that "something" became attraction. During the conference, Ethan and I were nearly inseparable. We sat next to one another at meals, attended many of the same breakout sessions, and spent time sharing all that we learned at the conference. I relished the time we spent together.

On our return trip, we were stranded in Nebraska due to a snowstorm that shut down the interstate. We found a comfortable hotel, and for two days we were stuck there. Ethan stayed in his room while the rest of the group hung out. I was perplexed. He'd spent hours talking and laughing with us and then, suddenly … solitude.

Within a few days of returning home, I found myself yearning to be with Ethan. I'd never felt anything like this in my life: desire so strong it felt like it could consume me. While standing at my kitchen sink, I dropped to my knees and pleaded with God to take it away. I knew these feelings were not congruent with a healthy marriage, and I didn't want to go anywhere with them. They went away—just like that. They were boxed up and put in a warehouse like the Ark of the Covenant in *Raiders of the Lost Ark*. The invasive, lascivious emotions were erased from my mind.

From that point on, while Ethan and I participated in playful banter and the occasional deep conversation, I no longer had the draw toward him that I had experienced during our road trip. As a volunteer, I was now intensely involved with our weekend services, performing or directing sketches, setting the theme through a personal monologue, or being the "welcome and announcements" girl. I was so intimately involved with the service that I was included in the programming meetings. Those meetings revealed a side of Ethan I hadn't seen before. He was gregarious and charismatic, but he could also be harsh and demanding. If anyone involved in the service disappointed him, he would say negative, hurtful things to or about them. Sometimes he told hysterical but demeaning jokes about people who displeased him. Even as I laughed, I'd be thinking, *Something about this isn't right.*

Due to his charisma and vision for bringing the message of Christ to the lost, hurting and broken, Ethan had a lot of people following him. His speaking style was raw, personal, and humorous. His teachings were intensely applicable to daily life. People adored him. They wanted to be his best friend, to be involved in his life, and to be liked by him. If they had known the things he was saying about them and the jokes he made at their expense, they would have been hurt but—sickeningly—I believe they would still have been drawn to him. Seeing "the real Ethan" and knowing what I knew made my stomach churn. However, let him flash a smile my way or give me a rare but weighty compliment, and I was drawn in by his charm—not in a romantic manner at this point but by his captivating magnetism.

In the summer of 2001, nearly four years after the road trip to Chicago, Ethan invited me to join the church staff and take on the programming coordinator position. Until that point, he had been filling that role, but as the church was nearing eighteen hundred people, it was becoming more difficult for him to continue all his responsibilities. I was passionate about seeing the church reach as many people as possible, and the job offer was a tremendous compliment. In addition to my passion, I had been working with Ethan long enough to see his negatives but to also appreciate his positive qualities. I was still seeking affirmation from him, and I gobbled up every crumb he tossed my way. Those crumbs left me wanting more.

Now on this December night in 2001, Ethan asked me to meet with him in private because we were experiencing some difficulties working together. Earlier in the week, he'd said he couldn't work with me anymore because I was a woman. I confronted him about that statement, because there were other women in the office with whom he had to interact. His claim seemed inconsistent; he asked me to come into his office to talk about it.

Ethan's office was warm and inviting. He didn't use the overhead fluorescent lights but preferred the muted illumination provided by a few lamps. From the door to his office there was a director's chair immediately to the right with the back pushed against the wall. Ethan's desk was next to the chair. There was a couch along the wall to the left of the entrance and a window on the opposite wall from the couch. As I entered Ethan's office I sat in the director's chair.

I pushed back in my chair, crossing one leg under the other in an attempt to get comfortable in the canvas director's chair placed strategically at the side of Ethan's desk. If I sat naturally, I would be facing out toward a wall; if I turned completely to my right, I could look Ethan in the eye. I turned to face him directly. "I just don't get it. You work with other women. What's the problem with me?"

"My problem isn't that you are a woman. My problem is that you are you."

Perplexed, I pushed for more. "What do you mean? Is there something wrong with me?"

"No." The word hung in the air, lingering like there was more to follow, but for the first time since I'd known him, he didn't seem to want to speak. He pushed his chair away from his desk and rolled it out until he was directly in front of me. I turned forward, to face him. "My problem is that I like you." He waited a moment before adding, "I'm attracted to you."

I swallowed hard, trying to seem composed, as if I was accustomed to hearing things like this. My peripheral vision got cloudy. I felt as if the room was closing in on me. *Did I just hear that correctly? He's attracted to me? To **me**?* Ethan had entered my warehouse and not only discovered the hidden Ark of the Covenant but opened it as well. All the feelings I had stuffed away four years earlier were released by Ethan's revelation.

He went on, "Remember when we were coming back from Chicago and we got stuck in Nebraska? I didn't come out of my room for two days. Do you know why?"

I shook my head, too shocked to speak.

"The time we spent talking and laughing as we drove across the country was more than just fun. I'm drawn to you. I admire you. You possess amazing talent. Your heart is tender toward God and those who don't know Him. There are parts of me that come alive when I'm with you. That's a problem. I had to hide—to stay away from you. I told my roommate, 'Don't let me leave this room or I might do something risky.' I didn't trust myself with you."

I shifted in my chair, trying to process what I had just heard and simultaneously appear as though I wasn't in shock. I was more than flattered. I had boxed away this connection not realizing that Ethan had felt the same way. Now I was discovering the truth and I relished hearing it. Suddenly that knowledge became quite intoxicating. I bathed in the revelation for a moment, soaking it in as an ingredient my soul longed for but had not experienced. I felt as though I was immersed in a gorgeous tub surrounded by rose petals. The focus was entirely on me. It was surreal.

It's not that I had never felt wanted, I was married after all. My husband had pursued me (not that I played all that hard to get). There was something different about Ethan being interested in me. Was it because we were both married? To be attractive on several levels to a man who technically was untouchable and shouldn't be doing any pursuing, is that what added to the intensity of his words? Did the fact that he was a pastor contribute to the magnitude of the taboo?

In the nanoseconds that passed, reason began to rise to the surface in my head, past the rose-filled tub and the longing to be admired. But my reasoning was slightly altered. I had, after all, enjoyed the previously dormant, exhilarating feelings Ethan's confession had revealed. Unfortunately, reason sounded like this: I confessed to Ethan that I was also attracted to him. I told him that although it seemed appropriate for me to quit in this context, I didn't want to because I loved what I was doing. The road trip connection had been boxed up and effectively ignored for four years, so I sincerely believed I could continue to keep it in check. Ethan didn't like the idea of not working with me and illogically reasoned as well that the best thing for us to do was continue working together. We both believed we could keep our feelings for each other under control and inconspicuous. At that point, neither one of us had any desire to leave our spouses and upset the balance in our carefully measured lives. Our jobs were high profile in our community, and neither of us would jeopardize them. It all seemed so cut and dry.

I can hear you saying something along the lines of, "You foolish, self-centered woman. What were you thinking?" Believe me, I frequently revisit this scene and ask myself the same question. However, admiration and pursuit are intoxicating. I have not come across a single person who doesn't want to be appreciated. The countless dollars that have been spent on hours of therapy to heal wounds left by caregivers who failed to appropriately encourage or praise children are a testament to this. Hardwired into each of us is the desire for authentic love, acceptance, and praise. Children will do whatever is necessary to receive even a grotesquely twisted version of these if that's all that is offered to them.

I drove away from work that night in a fog. As I meandered my way down the main highway heading west, my thoughts drifted far off the rural roads. I knew the roads well and didn't need to think about where I was going physically. My emotional journey required my full attention. I was on a road I had never traveled before, and I had no idea how to navigate it. Up to this point in my life, I had taken pride in pretty much knowing everything that seemed important to know. I loved being the go-to girl. This night I found myself in uncharted territory. For what seemed like the first time in my life, I had no idea what to do.

Thoughts of my husband galloped across my heart and my head. He's a decent man. I did not want to hurt him. In my state of utter ignorance regarding how to deal with this new journey, my thoughts turned to something I did know: pain and sadness. Even though I had little idea of how to handle Ethan's revelation, I believed that if I told my husband about my attraction to Ethan, it would devastate him.

The familiar streets of my old neighborhood snapped me back to where I was going. Minutes later, I sat in the trendy red living room of a friend who was hosting Friday-night Bunko. Bunko is a simple game using dice to score points. This particular Bunko game was a monthly gathering of neighborhood women. We would enjoy food, wine and conversation uninterrupted by children. My husband and I had moved away from the neighborhood a few years earlier but on occasion I was invited to Bunko to fill in for a regular who couldn't make it. I felt honored to be included even though I no longer lived there.

As I tossed my dice and casually chatted with the women at my table, I was curious if any of them had ever been in my situation. Being the one in the know and simultaneously aware of the indecency of it all, I certainly wasn't going to bring up this topic. At the time, it was very important for me to have it all together. Please notice I didn't write "appear to have it all together." No, I wasn't interested in the façade; I deeply wanted to be perfect. Perfection was how I got attention. It was how I was able, until that night, to feel good about myself and my contribution to society. Not only could I not ask questions about dealing with a man expressing interest in me, but I also could not even mention that this might be happening in my life. I could never open up about this to anyone.

I have no recollection of my Bunko achievements that night. I just remember feeling so different from every other woman in that room—walking in a forbidden realm and separate. In this strange and foggy state, I pulled into the garage of the home that I shared with my husband and three children. It was the very home my husband and I had visions of remodeling someday. We had thought of bumping out the living room and adding a bathroom, a bedroom, a sunroom, and a pool in the backyard. This home was a huge departure from the previous perfectly manicured neighborhood homes we had owned. The thought of living in a neighborhood that didn't have a strict homeowner's association appealed to us. We had traded covenant restrictions for unconstrained homeowner's freedom. Was this a precursor to what was beginning to happen in my own life?

As I sat pondering in the garage, I had a clear vision of my husband weeping. At that moment I solidified my decision to keep Ethan's revelation to myself. In my "enlightened" mind, I concluded this was the best solution. This is how I would protect my husband. With this resolve set firmly in my heart and mind, I walked gingerly into the darkened home. I quietly took my place under the cozy comforter next to my husband without an exchange of words—just a silent resolution to keep everything under control.

Chapter 2

Quest for Perfection

I AWOKE THE NEXT MORNING TO THE sound of laughter as it bounced from the kitchen, down the hall, to our bedroom. The source: my husband and our five-year-old son, Paul, the youngest of our three children. At the time, Paul was still cuddly and liked cozying up in my lap while we read stories or watched TV. Then, without notice, he would leap out of my arms to begin an assault on the imaginary enemies that had penetrated the fortress around our home. It was up to Paul to masterfully wield his sword and destroy every last one.

I lay in bed listening to the giggles streaming from Paul and the goofy talk of my husband, which just egged Paul on. I thought about the night before. Was it real? Had I just imagined all of it? After awakening fully, I sensed the weight of the truth pressing down on me. I wiggled my arms out from underneath the warmth of our down comforter to grab for my journal and a pen. I sat up just enough to be able to write but still keep as much of my body as possible enveloped in the warmth of the bed. I found my place in my journal and cryptically expressed my thoughts. I didn't think my husband read my journal, but I had to be evasive just in case he did. I couldn't keep these thoughts in my head. They yearned to be out, expressed in a way that was safe—in a way that was mine alone and that no one else could share.

I have kept journals for years. I started when I was a freshman in high school. My high school years were some of the most difficult of my life. I remember deciding to keep a journal for two reasons. Partly I had a burning to write and I savored the experience of watching my words flow out of me and onto paper. The other driving force was my fear of losing connection with my teenage self as I aged. It seemed that my mother didn't understand me or confess remembering the challenges of her growing-up years. I was so perplexed by this. How could anyone forget the horribleness of being a teenager? Maybe her teenage years were ideal. I don't know but I was aware of my fear of losing touch with that very real part of me and that time in my life. The fear fueled my decision to write it all down so the memories wouldn't be lost.

I grew up in Aspen, Colorado, in a hotel that my parents owned and operated. To save time and money, we lived there. My unique home provided a stimulating and variety-filled childhood. I was the fifth of six children born to my parents. I also have two foster sisters who take the oldest and the youngest positions in our family. Not only were there a lot of us, but there were also always people around. My childhood playground was a lobby filled with repeat guests who were like extended family.

My parents were preoccupied with building their business and catering to the guests. I was only rarely noticed by them. I knew I had to do well in school, and although I was a consistent A and B student, I did not receive life-giving praise from my parents. They were hardworking products of the Depression. They knew the value of an honest day's work and believed that their role as parents was to provide a roof over our heads, food in our mouths, and firm discipline. All of these needs are important, and they did an excellent job of filling them. However, what I longed to hear from them was their pride in me. I wanted them to notice me.

As a young girl, I sought ways to be noticed by anyone, and I involved myself in activities that might provide a means of attention. I was consistently trying something new, searching for my niche. I learned to ski when I was about five but let go of thoughts of being a professional ski racer when I discovered I was fearful of speed. I took gymnastics lessons after watching Nadia Comaneci score perfect tens at the Olympics. I tried my hand at skating and diving, as well as participating on the swimming and softball teams. Nothing seemed to fit. This search continued throughout my years growing up in Aspen.

Beginning in middle school, a desire to be accepted by my peers took root, blossoming into its fullness during high school. As a freshman, I began to make a name for myself in the theater department. I received favorable reviews in my first performance as an elderly woman with gigantic boobs, something I didn't possess even remotely (a defeating absence in the life of a teenage girl). I continued to perform in plays and musicals throughout high school, getting the occasional lead. I discovered another theatrical outlet as a member of the speech and debate team and thrived in the interpretation of poetry category. I performed decently, placing first several times with a script from *Spoon River Anthology*. Although this was rewarding, my yearning for acknowledgment was not quenched. In fact, I have little memory of my parents attending or even being interested in my theatrical achievements.

I feebly tried sports by joining the freshman basketball team. During that painfully long season from November through

March, I experienced a total of two minutes, forty-one seconds of actual court time. That's my combined total over the entire season. I remember one time getting the ball as a guard and not knowing which direction led to our basket. Thankfully, I never actually made any baskets since they were sure to have been points for the opposing team.

With my hopes of playing for the WNBA dashed completely, I optimistically turned to cheering on the athletic teams and tried out for cheerleading. As it happened, the day of tryouts coincided with the first day of my first period—ever. I had heard all about it in eighth-grade health class and figured out what to do all on my own. I never told my mom, and she never asked. I remember standing in the girls' locker room drying off my shorts in front of the hand dryer, hoping that I had removed any traces of the rite of passage that had taken place on that day. I wasn't comfortable with the changes of the female body and preferred to keep all signs of my humanity hidden. Beyond that, who wants to be on stage in front of the whole school doing the splits and high kicks with blood on her shorts?

I didn't make the cheerleading team that year, but my best friend did. My unrelenting drive to be noticed fueled a destructive jealousy toward her. As a result, I dismantled our relationship. I don't remember that I said anything directly to her. Doing so would have revealed a dark part of me; I wouldn't be perfect if I did that. Instead, I let her busyness with her new cheerleading friends be the excuse for not getting together with her. I'm sure my passive-aggressive side allowed my jealousy to leak out in indirect but obvious ways. I longed for attention and acceptance.

I made the cheerleading team the following year, but by then my former best friend had moved away. As a junior, I got the lead in the school musical, *Joseph and the Amazing Technicolor Dreamcoat*. I played the part of the Narrator. As a senior, I got the lead role in a dramatic stage production of *The Girl in the Mirror*. These accomplishments were somewhat soothing to my ego. I relished the opportunity to be on stage and entertain the audience; however, I'm not sure if my parents were there. I have a vague memory of my mom greeting me after *Joseph*, but that's it. They didn't attend sports events and see me cheering. I was doing really well but not good enough to be noticed.

To me, graduation day represented more than the completion of high school; it was release from captivity. I believed that college held the keys to finding my place in this world. I had a boyfriend off and on throughout high school. I was obsessively drawn to this young man, and it drove me crazy that he didn't consistently reciprocate those feelings. In the fall of my senior year, I started looking at colleges to attend. My mom suggested her alma mater, Bucknell University, which is located in central Pennsylvania. It was a good school and much closer to the cosmopolitan cities of the east. To impress my sometime-boyfriend, stand out from the crowd, and please my mom, that's where I went.

The choice did not have the desired effect with my boyfriend. He ended our relationship for the last time in December while I was home for the holidays during my freshman year. I was devastated, but at a fraternity party on my first night back at school for the spring semester, my hall-mate Rita introduced me to John. Initially I noticed John's enchanting blue eyes. The second facet that drew me toward this young man from New York was his unique sense of humor. With John's friend Tom, we headed to an upstairs living room, away from the noisy, beer-saturated party in the basement. We laughed and talked for hours. I remember thinking that night how odd it was that I felt comfortable with John so quickly. Why was that? A few weeks later, after our first date, we spent hours talking and kissing in the stairwell of my dorm. He felt warm and cozy, like my favorite jammies. His lips were soft and inviting. I fell for him immediately and was shocked that I could shift so quickly from depression about losing my high school beau to infatuation with someone else.

Our relationship blossomed as John and I continued to discover one another. For the remaining year and a half before he graduated, we spent countless hours in the cafeteria talking about our respective childhoods and laughing about everything. We would have the occasional debate, which inspired John's heart to beat. He welcomed the opportunity to argue and would sometimes play devil's advocate just to incite me. A trait of his that I never grew to appreciate. Religious beliefs occasionally crept their way into our discussions. I had grown up going to church and chose to be baptized when I was twelve. I believed what I learned in church, and I read my Bible regularly, though I really didn't begin to understand it until I was in my mid-twenties. John had not discussed religion with someone he respected before me. He alleged that followers of Christ were brainwashed, having checked their intelligence at the door. I never thought of myself as particularly intelligent, but he did. His bias toward Christians was challenged, and our discussions were the catalyst to his journey of faith.

When John graduated from college, a promising job took him to San Francisco. Though it was challenging and difficult at times, we managed the long-distance relationship fairly well. Within a year, John's loneliness and disappointment with his job motivated him to move back to the east so we could be closer. After I finished my bachelor's degree in psychology at Bucknell a semester early in December of 1987, I took a job working as a research assistant at the National Institutes of Health in Bethesda, Maryland. By this time John was living in northern Maryland, an hour from Bethesda. We continued to date until 1989, when we got married. Marrying John seemed so natural. I felt safe with him. We got along well, he was a responsible and stable man, and we were still together after four and a half years. We enjoyed watching movies, occasional bike rides, and camping. We didn't participate in a plethora of activities together but that wasn't an issue for us. Getting married seemed like the logical next step in our lives.

I yearned to return to Colorado after my venture out east proved unsatisfying. I missed my family, the climate, and the beauty of home. When John proposed to me just before Christmas in 1988, I suggested we move to Aspen after our wedding and manage my parents' hotel. John agreed. We were married in September 1989. It was a beautiful time to get married in Aspen. The aspen trees had begun their magical transformation from green to gold, and the contrast of the evergreens and red oak brush created a spectacular backdrop for our celebration. We moved seamlessly from boyfriend and girlfriend to husband and wife. We escaped the usual issues of newly married couples. In fact, I couldn't understand what the big deal was about transitioning into married life. It was all very simple for us.

Managing my parents' hotel, however, was not simple. We lived behind the front office in one room and had very little privacy. We were at the guests' beck and call every night of the week. In addition, the frustration of working for my dad—who knew exactly how he wanted everything done and expected us to carry out his plans to a T—was more than I could handle. By the end of the ski season in 1990, John and I knew we were not cut out for the hotel business and resigned our positions. We moved to the Front Range, where John could continue his engineering career, and I went back to school to pursue a teaching certificate.

Before I finished my coursework, we conceived our first child. Although I treasured being pregnant, I wasn't entirely comfortable with this rite of passage. Much like my experience as a teenager when I transformed into woman, I didn't spend time talking about being pregnant or pampering myself. At times I denied the reality of my pregnancy and acted like nothing was different. When each of my three children was born, I detached the process of labor from its end result. I remember the labor and delivery nurse encouraging me to push when I had Paul. Because our first two children were girls, she was convinced he was a girl and kept saying, "Come on. You can do it. Let's get little Molly out so you can hold her in your arms." However, I never connected the pain and exertion to seeing or holding my baby. When I remember this, sadness and regret linger where connection and wholeness should have been.

Something was broken inside of me, a fact of which I was not aware at the time. Somehow my disconnected nature was expressed to the world as a person who could handle anything. At four weeks old, our first child, Anna, was diagnosed with cystic fibrosis. Commonly referred to as CF, the genetic disorder primarily affects the lungs and digestive system, resulting in low weight gain and compromised lung function. Although I was saddened by the thought of losing my newborn, I moved quickly into what-do-we-do-now mode. I handled her daily treatments and regular two-week hospital stays like they were just a part of life. I didn't cry; I was strong. In fact, sometimes I would have to hold back a smile when I heard she would need to be hospitalized. It was like my emotions were reversed. I wouldn't feel sad. I felt awkwardly happy.

Immediately after our second child, Grace, was born, I hemorrhaged. The doctor couldn't get the bleeding to cease. I was matter-of-fact throughout the entire ordeal. I knew there was a problem and was aware of being put under general anesthesia for a D&C to remove any lingering placenta that might be the cause. I remember coming out of it and hearing the first procedure didn't work and going under again for an arterial ligation and possible hysterectomy if the ligation wasn't successful. When the doctor first announced the problem, John didn't know what to do. He turned to me for help. I coolly told him to call my family and tell them to pray. *I* was not connected to the reality of *my* situation. This disconnected state provided me with the ability to calmly deal with the gravity of the situation, but I don't believe it testifies to being an integrated person.

I see this disconnect as a byproduct of my desire to be perfect. Perfect people are unscathed by life's trials, appearing untouched and pulled together. Perfect people are the rocks others turn to in their time of need. Perfect people always feel great because they have no idea what they are genuinely feeling. My striving for perfection was applauded not only by my parents but by the world around me as well. This unconscious façade proved to be the ingredient that drew people toward me and temporarily satisfied my yearning for acceptance. Another way to describe this is with the words people-pleaser and co-dependent. Basically a co-dependent is a people-pleaser whose definition of self comes from the thoughts, actions, and words of others.

When Grace was one, John and I got involved with a group of people from our church who set out to replicate an emerging concept: the seeker-friendly church. We designed relevant, engaging, grace-filled church services to draw in the individual seeking for answers to the Bible, God, and Jesus, with no condemnation or pressure to conform into the image of someone like Dana Carvey's "Church Lady." While I genuinely wanted to support a church that I could invite friends to, there was a danger in it that I was unaware of: a new church with a lot of needs is generally the downfall for a people-pleaser. For several years I immersed myself in the church. I was busy with three children, caring for our home, and volunteering for any need that arose. I found meaning and purpose for my life by parenting my kids and giving my time to a worthy cause. I was busy and tired, but I had it all together.

Although I had a lot going on, I treasured the moments I had with my kids. Bedtime was especially sweet. I would read them stories, sing songs, and then tuck each one in with a prayer, a kiss, and an, "I love you." One night Grace asked me if her daddy and I would ever get divorced. I don't recall what precipitated the question. Perhaps a friend's parents were going through a divorce, or perhaps John and I had a very rare argument. Whatever the reason, I knew I could confidently dissuade her fear. I responded with a solid, "Never!" When she asked me the same question several years later, my answer was a crestfallen, "I don't know."

Chapter 3

Emerging Deception

I REMEMBER WHEN I WAS YOUNG, MAYBE seven years old, I used to steal money from our babysitter. She had a room in the part of our hotel where we lived. I don't remember why she was there, just that she was. She slept in an antique brass bed that seemed to stand three feet off the ground, with a cavern of space underneath that was big enough for a large coin jar. She must have put spare change in it. I don't know what its significance was; all I knew was that it contained money. I would periodically sneak under the bed and carefully remove some coins. I wanted to be sure it wasn't obvious that coins were being carried away because I didn't want to alert her that one of us was a thief. After smoothing the coins to look as though nothing was out of place, I would quickly stuff the goods into my pockets and hurry to my room to add to the stash of money I was collecting. Stealing felt wrong, but I also knew I would be able to get what I wanted because of it: diapers and a bottle for my Baby Alive. My pleasure seeking as a young girl, though less destructive than in my adult years, was a precursor of the things to come. Like most people, I appeared to be angelic but could also be deceptive.

One aspect of humanity I didn't understand as a young girl is that we are all capable of both kind acts and hurtful ones. I wanted to believe I was only good. In fact, I assumed that I had to be only good, so the deceit was something I stuffed away. I unconsciously chose not to connect with that part of me and sincerely believed I was good all the time.

Locked into my memory is a snapshot of what I now believe was a pivotal point in developing my hidden self. In my memory, my siblings and I are standing in a row facing my dad, who has my oldest sister in his grip. He is preparing to use his belt to spank her. For years that snapshot has popped unannounced into my memory. At one moment I'm just going about my day and the next the snapshot flashes across my mind and then disappears. No emotions travel with the snapshot. All my life, I have thought nothing of it. Once, out of curiosity, I asked my oldest sister what that scene was about. She told me she had forgotten to take out the trash, and while the memory seemed to hold little emotion for me, she was traumatized by the experience. She was humiliated in front of her siblings to teach all of us a lesson: do what you're told or you will feel pain.

I'm not picking on my dad. Spankings were a rare occurrence in our home because we knew dad would follow through on his threat to discipline us. My dad believed his actions were right and just. It was the way he was raised and it worked. He wanted us to be well-behaved children, and corporal punishment was an effective tool. At least on the surface, we were good kids; however, fear and physical punishment did not address the desires that motivated less-than-acceptable behavior. What we learned from this type of management was how to hide our true selves and not get caught. If part of me was unacceptable to someone, I would do whatever was necessary to avoid exposing that part. I developed this behavior into a strong protective mechanism that served me well. Until my affair began, I had yet to discover just how much deception I was capable of containing.

⸺

The next time Ethan and I saw one another, relief replaced the thick tension that had once hung over us like an intangible fog. As the sun broke through, a hint of mist remained in the form of awkwardness. I wasn't exactly sure how to conduct myself around a man who had confessed both his attraction to me and his intention to keep the magnetism under control.

Later that day, I cautiously approached Ethan's office to talk about an upcoming service we were working on together. The smile on Ethan's face as I peered through his doorway and the way he lit up put my anxiety at ease. As I stepped into Ethan's office, he stood up to close the door behind me. I slipped into the chair beside his desk—the director's chair. It was not particularly comfortable, but it was the very chair I sat in the night Ethan confessed his true feelings for me. Not only did this chair provide the closest physical proximity to Ethan, but it also held the memory from just a few nights before. We talked about how good it felt to see one another again and the relief we both enjoyed now that we knew where we stood with one another. As the conversation continued, I eased into what I believed would become our manner of relating to one another: honesty as we had shared our deep feelings for one another and understanding that those feelings would be held at bay. We would not support the natural progression of attraction expressed. Without realizing it, we had embarked on a journey that is rarely navigated with success.

In the next few weeks, my schedule began filling up due to marathon meetings with Ethan. We would meet with a team on a regular basis, but Ethan always found reasons for the two of us to have private meetings—meetings that lasted three hours at times. Mostly we spent our time talking about our views on pop culture and the latest edition of *People* magazine. Staying on top of societal norms and who's who in the entertainment industry seemed to be pertinent to the type of church services we were organizing. Humor and casual conversation were focal points of our meetings. For Ethan, who was intensely stressed by the challenges of keeping pace with a growing church, our meetings provided the light comic relief he desperately sought. Ethan relaxed around me, and I got satisfaction from that fact. For me, it was gratifying just to be chosen to fill this unique role in his life.

At this time, Ethan and I were working intensely on a Christmas Eve service. We spent hours putting the event together, but it seemed to take twice as long as it should to get everything done. Ethan and I were spending so much of our work time hanging out together in his office that I had to pack a tremendous amount of work into just a few hours. I began making many calls to my husband saying I would be late getting home. I didn't feel guilty about making the calls. I did not connect emotionally with what was going on in my relationship with Ethan and the resulting slow deterioration of my ties to my children and husband.

The night of the Christmas Eve services was electric. Everything came off without a hitch, just as I had hoped. Ethan's growing approval of me rested in part on the outcome of this service. The impact we had hoped to make was achieved. It was an environment that invited people to consider who Christ is, why He came here, and the direct connection of Him to their lives. The excitement was so thick in the air that I could have jumped right into Ethan's arms to hug him and celebrate all that had taken place that night. It would have been authentic but not neutral, so I kept my physical distance, which was awkward. Normally I would have given Ethan that hug. Instead we stood in the back of the room in awe of all that had transpired that night, including the work that led up to the event. It was our own quiet way of celebrating, all the while wishing we could fall into one another's arms and relish the thrill of the night.

A somber haze attached to the celebratory mood reminded me of the meaning of the event. It was about remembering the night our Savior was born—a Savior who, in His later years, spoke of living an honest life and maintaining our commitments. He also said we would be unable on our own to live up to that standard, and He came to bridge the gap between the expectation and our ability. I was entering into a realm in which I would begin to understand the distance between me and God more fully than I had ever thought possible. Missing at this point was my realization not only of the danger of my growing attraction to Ethan but also of the hallowed ground on which I stood.

Ethan and I wrapped up the night. As some of the last few to leave the auditorium, we headed outside to join our respective families. Emptiness began to replace the jubilation of the night as the realization that Ethan was heading out of town for the holidays with his family slid its way into my mind. Just outside the main doors, his wife and children were tucked carefully into their car, ready to begin a well-deserved getaway. As we headed out into the crisp December air, I casually said good-bye to Ethan and his family. I pretended I was excited for them, but deep down I wished I was the one strapped into the seat next to Ethan.

The next afternoon, I received a call from a coworker informing me that Ethan had been in an accident. Immediately, the blood drained out of my head; I felt it pool somewhere in my stomach, stopping in my throat on the way. A sinking sensation began to envelop me and I felt myself drifting away. As the details unfolded,

I slowly came back to reality. Though the accident he had been in was life threatening, miraculously, Ethan was not dead. In fact, he sustained only minor injuries.

I was relieved to hear that Ethan was going to be OK, but I was simultaneously hurt that he had not called me himself. I wanted to hear his voice, to know for certain that he was not gravely injured. I experienced another feeling as well. As a bolt shot through my body, I recognized it as the fear of God. I snapped fully into the awareness of the danger of my increasing draw toward Ethan. I was convinced that in some way this was a warning and that Ethan was being punished for our relationship. Fear had been a strong motivating presence in my life growing up. I hated pain, physical or emotional, and would do whatever was necessary to avoid it. I strengthened my resolve not to pursue more than a friendship with Ethan.

The relationship that Ethan and I developed by this time would best be described as an emerging emotional affair. We had crossed boundaries by spending extended time together and filling small roles that were meant for our spouses. I didn't recognize how close I was growing to Ethan, but my disappointment that he hadn't called me himself to tell me about his accident testified to my guilt.

Within a few days, I received the longed-for call from Ethan. I was thrilled to hear his voice, and I doubt that I contained my enthusiasm. I headed to the basement to take the call so I could talk freely with Ethan. I asked about his accident and how he was doing. He filled me in on the details and sounded thankful that I cared—and I did. I soothed him with my words of interest and concern. This was a trait that naturally emerged from me anytime someone I knew had a need, and Ethan was not an exception. I liked that I knew how to be there for someone. Later, when my husband asked me to whom I was talking, I told him it was

Ethan and that he was just going over some future service ideas with me.

Ethan returned from his getaway, and we picked up where we left off. We were working closely on service planning and taking a lot of time to accomplish our tasks. During that winter, Ethan's mom got very sick. Again, I got to be there for him. I listened as he expressed his concerns about his mom's health. To the best of my ability, I felt his pain with him and tried to anticipate ways that I could best support him. When it was clear that his mom probably would not make it, he headed home to be with her. While he was gone, we talked on the phone frequently. I listened more than I talked, and Ethan expressed his thankfulness for our friendship.

I sent a bouquet of tulips, symbolic of the emerging spring, and a colorful respite from the darkness of death that surrounded Ethan's mom. I sent cards of encouragement to her, hoping to shed rays of hope into the fearful twists and turns on her journey away from this earth. Ethan thanked me for every action and complimented me on my compassion toward both his mother and him. While the part of me I was in touch with fully believed my motives were pure, a part of me that I was less aware existed knew this was moving in an unhealthy direction. The naive part of me didn't tell my husband what I was doing. I didn't even think about it.

When Ethan's mom passed away a few weeks later, he told me how he longed for me to be the one beside him as he put her in a body bag, waited for the coroner to pick her up, attended her funeral, and met with family. His words were honey to my heart. I licked them up, savoring every last sweet drip. I wasn't seeking these praises; they were being doled out because I was just being myself. Because I was pouring my attention into Ethan during the painful loss of his mom, I felt needed by him, and he let me in to his heart.

The closeness between us was intensifying. We talked at times about our feelings for one another. We addressed the physical intensity that was exacerbated by our intention not to cross the line. We thoughtlessly started talking about how good it might feel to hold one another and fulfill our deeply held longings.

In addition to being the programming coordinator at the church, I was also the women's ministry leader. Ironically, I was putting together a women's retreat and dealing with the indiscretions of a young single woman who was to be our emcee. She had disclosed to me that she and a friend had recently had sex. She didn't quite know why, and her actions really bothered her. She believed it was not appropriate to be involved with the retreat and disqualified herself. I compassionately agreed with her and took on her role as emcee. I was so disconnected from the part of me that was having an emotional affair that I didn't hesitate to take over.

As weeks and months passed, Ethan and I continued to maintain our physical distance. My husband and I were doing well. We had always gotten along, rarely arguing. Since our lives centered on our children, meals, and work, we spent very little time together as a couple. Neither one of us complained. We were content—at least I had been content before Ethan. One of the topics of my conversation with Ethan focused on John's shortcomings. Ethan pointed out to me that John was not a feeler. Being very logically minded, John didn't take into account matters of the heart. While this was partially true, I swallowed it whole. I allowed Ethan's comments to create a shift in the way I viewed my husband. I now noticed every time he stepped into the logical, cognitive realm without connecting to my emotional needs—needs I had been oblivious to prior to my conversations with Ethan.

At the same time, I loved my husband. As a result of roads he had not taken, he was mildly depressed for most of our marriage. He was a talented musician but chose a different career path, fearful that music would never pay the bills—logical thinking. I often suggested he quit his job and find a better fit. In fact, the reason I was working at the church was to provide for our family so John could finally pursue the music degree he had always wanted. He had been taking classes for a year, and I sensed his depression creeping back in. On one of our rare nights out together, I asked him about it. He realized that the degree he was pursuing wasn't the answer. He wanted to be a performer. Since he had a family and we lived far from the music industry headquarters, he believed his desire was just a pipe dream. He was letting it go.

I was sad for John. I wanted good things in his life. I wanted him to find a job that gave his passion a place to flourish, but it seemed that was never going to happen. A part of me died that night. Previously I had a flicker of hope that he might finally find contentment in his job, but I realized I had to let go of that. No longer could I be his cheerleader. There was nothing to cheer him toward. I thought I had found purpose in bringing life to John, but I had failed. As the flame died, one last glimmer of light popped into my head that night: I would take him to Italy for a surprise Christmas gift. John's Italian roots and passion for espresso inspired the destination. It would be the once-in-a-lifetime trip that I was sure would cheer him up.

John was without words on Christmas day when he opened a travel book to Italy, along with tickets and our itinerary. He looked up as if to say, "Italy? We're really going to Italy!" The magic was already at work. My mom came a few weeks later and watched our kids, so it was just the two of us in Italy, the country of wine, art, and romance. Though we soaked up every bit of history, art, and good food, something was missing. I looked at the amazing sculptures and paintings depicting love, passion, and excellence and desired to have the same in my marriage. Our mealtimes were quiet, and I fought to create conversation with John. We stayed in romantic hotels in Rome and Florence but made love once, at most twice, during our getaway. Sadness and discontent began to wiggle their way into my heart and mind. As I soaked in the sights of Italy, I began to long for Ethan to be at my side. I knew that if he were with me, we would have hours-long discussions in the romantic cafés, kiss, and hold hands as we strolled along the cobblestone streets and marveled at the rich history depicted in the art and architecture. Ironically, Italy created a shift in my heart, not in John's.

After my Italy experience, life at work with Ethan became more and more satisfying and life at home became less so. While on vacation with our family in May 2003, John and I were hanging out by the pool. I was reading a book called *His Needs, Her Needs,* and I casually asked John if he would read the book with me. He didn't see the point. His comment seared the realization into my mind and heart that Ethan was right about him. John wasn't interested in the important emotional dimensions of life. I hadn't paid much attention to that part of myself in my disconnected state, so prior to Ethan's revelation, John's lack of interest didn't bother me. Since the fateful trip to Italy, however, it was all I could see. I didn't push the issue. I accepted it as the final nail in the coffin of my heart.

Once I returned from my family vacation, Ethan asked if we could meet for breakfast, and I eagerly agreed. I had so much to tell him about my disappointment with John and his disinterest in pursuing my heart. Meeting with Ethan was easy. Instead of heading straight to work, we met up at a restaurant. We talked and laughed, filling up every minute of our breakfast together with rich conversation, the kind that is so enjoyable time is lost. As we began to part ways in the parking lot, Ethan asked if I would like to go for a ride with him. *Sure,* I thought, *why not?* As I sat next to him, he gingerly held my hand. This was the first time either one of us had touched the other in a romantic way. His touch was soft, caressing, and electric. My heart was leaping for joy, and passion began to radiate throughout my body—from a handhold. If this was what it was like for Ethan to hold my hand, I began to imagine he was very good at expressing his love physically.

Chapter 4

Nursing Home Secrets

I CLUNG WITHOUT SHAME TO THE ALIBI that Ethan and I were just friends. We shared a lot in common, which led to longer and more frequent conversations. He would even call me at home on my cell. It's not unusual for a boss to call his right-hand person at home … right? We always had business to deal with, even on our days off.

Emotional and physical affairs—are they really that different? Somehow to me, maintaining that our relationship was *just* emotional made it and me seem less truant. If I crossed the physical boundary line with Ethan, then I was completely guilty. An emotional affair was easier to swallow. But it wasn't the truth, and I knew it. Even with the reality that I was involved in a relationship that had gone beyond the norms for someone who is married, I still tried to hide.

One night I came home from work around midnight, a good two hours later than I was expected. I got ready for bed, and as I exited the bathroom, my husband, who was in bed and I thought asleep, asked me what was going on. My back against the wall, I slipped down into a seated heap on the floor. I had been caught. I pulled my legs close to my chest. So much of me wanted to reveal the truth and be free of the bondage I was feeling then. In one of those moments when things can turn suddenly, I found myself explaining that Ethan and I had been working in the office when the cleaning team entered with a homeless man. He had found his way to the church, hoping for a place to sleep that night. I continued that we all worked together to help this very needy man find a place to stay for the night. This was true; however, it didn't take that long.

No, Ethan and I had spent about an hour and half of that two hours dancing on the line of physical intimacy. You know that feeling when you actually kiss and touch for the first time? The electricity was so intense and oh so wrong. I would swing from, "This is amazing!" to "What am I doing?" but the pull to walk away was strangled. It was like the cartoons where the person in a compromising situation has a devil on one shoulder and an angel on the other. They are both trying to pull the person toward their way of thinking. Let's just say my angel was annihilated.

My poor husband. He was baffled. He knew in his heart I was lying, but he didn't want to believe it. It was so out of character for me. But isn't that the way it is so often? So out of character? We hear it frequently on the news: "My son would never have been the one to open fire at his school." "My daughter would never hurt a flea. Besides, she loved that baby more than anyone on earth!" "He was always so by the book. There's no way he embezzled all that money. There must be another explanation." Hmmm … are we all really that together? Are all of us ticking time bombs? Are we just "one missed step" away from tanking our lives?

My husband's confusion led him to look for any evidence he could find. That evidence turned out to be my journal. I ratted myself out. I didn't realize that I had been so blatant in there. I thought I had been cryptic. Somewhere along the journey, I began to be much more direct. I believe that a part of me really wanted out. Maybe I got more explicit in the hope that I might be rescued. My husband found an entry that read, "Ethan completes me," among others, that made it clear that I had moved beyond a friendship and into an affair. He confronted me with this information. I felt so interrogated. He was demanding and angry. I understand it now, but at the time I was shocked. How could he be so mad at me? My response to his anger was, "Oh my gosh, you are so overreacting." I told him that our relationship was just emotional and that nothing had happened between us. It's amazing how quickly I played stupid. "What are you talking about? It was in my head; it wasn't reciprocated." I took all the blame.

The fact was that Ethan and I had blatantly crossed physical boundaries. In the moments of passion, the thought that what I was doing was wrong was intertwined, vine-like, with utter pleasure seeking. It was clear to me. I just didn't have the strength to battle the pleasure-seeking strand. It was stronger than any pull I had ever experienced. For the first time in my life, I believed I was enjoyed from my head to my toes. I was told I was beautiful and thoroughly enjoyable. I craved the attentiveness and the words of passion dripping on me with every statement. It was absolutely addicting. I became captivated and felt that there was no way out once our relationship crossed that line.

We were creative in our rendezvous. A business park under construction in the evening, a lookout point during the day, mostly deserted dirt roads, even a Park 'n Ride, provided locations where we could get completely tangled with one another and for a moment forget about the reality of our situation. Ethan took periodic "study breaks" where he would hole up in a hotel for a few days to prepare for talks he would be giving. Those breaks provided us with the closest experience of what it might mean to be together. We would lie on the bed, perhaps his head resting on my knee, freely sharing dreams we had together. It was our version of pillow talk, and I treasured those moments.

There's a book in the Bible called the Song of Songs. It's all about a couple going through the seasons of love: dating, the desire to put action to their passion, the wedding night … I never really grasped the full meaning of Solomon's words until I experienced them first hand with Ethan. There was one very key ingredient missing: commitment and the reality that we were both married to other people. It ate at me repeatedly that although we had these amazing trysts filled with passion and intimacy, there was zero hope of commitment. In the heat of the moment, I thought I could leave my husband for Ethan. He was, it seemed, everything I wanted. But Ethan did not express the same thought, so at that time I didn't tell him mine.

After one of our interludes, as we lay intertwined on the bed, Ethan leaned up on one arm and said he wanted our relationship details to remain as a nursing home secret. I needed clarification. He told me he wanted this to remain something we never mentioned to anyone—to keep the physical aspect of our relationship a secret that we would carry with us to our death beds. He wanted to know that even in a nursing home, facing our last days on earth, we would not tell anyone of the passion and depth of what we shared. My heart sank at that very moment. I was fully in. I was giving all of myself to this man, and he was telling me that we would never be together and that all of this was just between us.

I allowed the pain to linger for a moment and then boxed it away. I thought, *OK, if he can do that, then so can I.* I began thinking about the people who might at that very moment be sitting in rocking chairs carrying their own nursing home secrets. I warmed up to the idea that this was all we would ever share, enamored with the mystery of it. It was something I was able to deal with at times, and at others I would find myself in utter despair, realizing I was making a mistake. A nagging thought hovered about me that this was not what I was created for. It was a thought that at times gave me strength to walk away but would then slip silently through my heart and out into the shadows surrounding me.

I often hear and read that when a relationship becomes physical, it is much harder to pull away from that person, even if being with him or her is not ultimately healthy. It answers, in part, why so many of us stay with a person despite unhealthy relational patterns and mismatched connections. I know it seems archaic to stay out of bed with our love interests we are not married to, but I get it. It's not an easy road to travel, but honestly, think about the relationships you've been involved in that went on far too long—the ones you knew you shouldn't be in, that weren't right for you, but you stayed anyway. Or think about the unhealthy relationships you tried to end repeatedly but kept going back to out of loneliness or despair. You didn't really want to be with that person; you just didn't want to be alone. I will bet with 99 percent accuracy (there's always an exception!) that you were involved physically. We cross that line and become intertwined. Leaving that person and ending the relationship has been described as a violent ripping apart of two souls that were joined through physical intimacy. If you haven't experienced it, good! It is utter pain, something I wouldn't even wish on an enemy.

My nursing home secret with Ethan was just another thread strengthening the cord of hiding. Not only was I fearful of revealing what was really going on, but Ethan was asking for the very same: just keep it all in the darkness. Unfortunately, or fortunately, my husband's discovery of my incriminating journal entries let at least a portion of the cat out of the bag.

After my husband confronted me with his discovery, he asked me what I was going to do. I knew at that point that I didn't want anyone to know what had happened. I really wanted to protect Ethan, the church, and myself, so I told him I would quit my job. I didn't want to, but it seemed clear to me that was the sacrifice I was going to have to make. Had it really come to this?

Chapter 5

The End of Dreams

I LOVED MY JOB. IT WAS CHALLENGING and mentally stimulating. No day was like the one before. It was the adventure I had been created for, and I felt very alive. Beyond the fact that I was having an affair, I loved the people I worked with. It was energizing to work with a team, to encourage people to give their best, and to be in relationships that were linked together with a common goal. I had purpose and meaning, and I was valued.

It may be hard to believe, but while I was having an affair, I was simultaneously dedicated to what God was doing in and through the church. I never lost that focus. I prayed sincerely before every service for God's hand to move in the hearts of the people who were there. I became increasingly more empathic toward those who were in less-than-perfect situations. I was gaining an understanding of what it meant to want to do the right thing but to continually bash your head against a wall and make no progress. I got what Paul was saying in Romans 7. I do what I don't want to do, and I don't do what I want to do. I was not, as some may have thought, totally on the side of the devil. I was foolish but not evil. It is entirely possible to love God, to try to follow Him, and to be screwing things up all at the same time. I get that.

At this point, no one knew why I quit my job. I told people that working had pulled me away from my family (true) and that I needed to focus my attention on home, not work (also true). So much was left unsaid in that space after the period. I looked like a saint. Revolting! I had a teary, heart-warming "last day at work" celebration. My coworkers said all kinds of sweet things to me, I got a few parting gifts, and everyone seemed sorry to see me go. That's the perfect ending—the plastic, artificial façade that is so prevalent in our culture and so far from reality. Behind it a load of crap remains hidden in the dark. How does any of the façade create bridges or healing?

Because I had left on such good terms, I was still part of the team as a volunteer. I could participate in weekend services when they needed me and fill in when my replacement was out of town (facades can be convenient). That lasted for about seven months. By this point, I was still secretly seeing Ethan. My husband could read right through my lies. The next tattler he turned to were the cell phone bills. They do not lie. With proof in hand, this time my husband went straight to the top—the ones who had the power to remove Ethan from his position, the elders. Their job is to protect the church. If I wouldn't stop seeing Ethan, then my husband was going to stop Ethan.

The plan sort of backfired. Instead of Ethan being asked to resign, my husband and I were requested to leave. The church we had helped start was now asking us to walk away. I was stunned. "You mean to tell me that you are going to keep Ethan in his position, teaching, after he told you he wasn't going to stop seeing me, and to somehow correct the problem, I have to leave? Seriously?" We were figuratively kicked out the door.

This was our home. We had committed countless hours of time to the foundation and building of this church. It's where our entire support system was. It was a huge connection for our kids. It was ... no longer ours. Another dream buried.

There was no team of people set up to surround us in our time of need, to help us work on our marriage, to offer strength to walk away from Ethan, or for me to be accountable to. Nope, nothing. They just sent us away. Now, if I had been hunting Ethan down, tempting him, luring him away from his work and family, I think I can understand the elders' approach. The truth was that the relationship was entirely two-sided. Ethan was as guilty as I was. I do not believe I would have pursued him. He started the pursuit; I just jumped right in and joined him. It is my understanding that we were and are equally guilty. So why just punish me? I think one word sums it up: fear. I think the elders were afraid, just as I was, that if Ethan was not at the church, it would fall. That's a very dangerous place to go—allowing the success of anything, but especially a church, to rest on the shoulders of one person instead of God. The fact that the church is thriving today is a testament not to a person but to God.

During the summer after we left the church, I decided it was time to come clean with my family. I drove to Aspen with my kids. They loved seeing their cousins, and nothing about going to Aspen seemed out of the ordinary. For me, everything was out of the ordinary. I never had big news to tell. I never needed to confess anything to my parents. As far as I was concerned, there had never before been anything to confess. I didn't have trips to the principal, and I didn't have to serve detention. This whole concept was so unfamiliar to me; not only unfamiliar, uncomfortable. I hated disappointing people, and by now I had done a lot of it.

My dad, a remarkable man I love deeply, is one of those people who seems to think he has it all figured out. At least that is how he comes across. When it comes to God, he talks like he knows what all of us should be doing, especially when we're not following God's plan. While growing up, I remember he used fear as a means of control. He lives and expects others to live in a very confined space—as if spirituality can be put in a box.

God just can't be put in a box, and neither can we. Yes, God is all good, and in His goodness, He created beings with free will. We have the capacity for both good and bad. We are not either black or white; we can fluctuate. We are whole beings. To put the fear of God in someone to control him or her to the point of denying his or her humanity is to control God in some way.

God is grace and truth, not fear. Yes, in the Old Testament fear was a huge motivator, but that was when humanity was under the law. We are now under grace, living in the age of grace. We have been for about two thousand years ... since Christ. Some people are fearful of grace. I think my dad was. It's scary to some to have so much freedom. We keep ourselves in tight little boxes with strict rules we can check off as we keep them, a measurement of sorts. We seem to find safety in that. Imprisonment is what it really is, and it was never what God intended.

God set basic rules for our preservation. We are supposed to live in enjoyment of all the good God has given us and not to judge. God's intention is for us to live under His authority (truth), but there's so much more about freedom and less about me staying in the box. I'm so thankful God has used this experience to help me grow in my understanding of who I really am and who He is. I wouldn't want someone to follow in my footsteps. If there's a less painful way to learn these things, go for it! Really!

As I revealed what had been going on, my parents were in disbelief and extremely disappointed. I had completely let them down. They both made repair attempts on me, trying desperately to fix their broken daughter with verses or statements. My mom told me I would never be happy again if I left my husband. Never! She told me I wasn't cute anymore. My dad read a verse to me about sheep going to heaven and goats going to hell. He said I was now a goat and would not be going to heaven when I died. I was headed for eternal damnation. I asked them if all the things I had done in the past that they thought were good counted for anything. They answered, "No." Just like that?

When my dad told me I was going to hell and my mom said I wasn't cute anymore, I realized the very things I had feared growing up were true. My parents' acceptance of me *was* dependent on my performance. The words stung more painfully than a whole swarm of bees. My very soul was pierced in such a way that I could not withstand it. I stood up, went inside, and told my kids it was time to go. By this point, we were ready to head home anyway. I took care of the last details of our long journey home with tears spilling down my cheeks. My kids asked what was wrong, and I told them. I explained that though Nana and Papa are kind people, they do not have the capacity to love their own daughter in her failings. At that moment, I realized I could not repeat the cycle. I added some new phrases to my vocabulary. On that very painful drive home, I heaved myself out from under the heavy burden of perfection. I told my children in as plain a way possible that no matter what they did, I would love them.

"So, even if I kill someone?" Yep, even if you kill someone, it won't matter. My love for you will not change. If you decide to sell your body to support a meth addiction, I'll still love you. I won't agree with your decision to sell your body, do drugs, or kill people, but your actions can't eradicate my love for you. I'll come and visit you in prison. You'll still have to pay the consequences of your decision. I won't give you money to buy drugs, but I'll take you out to lunch and love on you the best way I can. I will never shun you for your choices.

Tears were pouring out of my eyes as I realized that what I was saying to my kids were the very words I so desperately wanted to hear from my parents. And I didn't … still haven't, actually. Life has settled down since that swirling hurricane in 2004, and it's kind of like it never happened. I got back on track, married a stable guy my parents approve of, and keep my heart centered on him. That somehow seems to be enough, but I know that it's not OK with me to be loved for my performance.

Prior to this experience, I thought I had an idyllic childhood. I thought my parents were the most level-headed, balanced people in the world. I took pride in the fact that they have called me less than ten times in my entire life, thinking that was normal. I gained some useful skills from them, they taught me a lot, and I am grateful for them but they were and are far from perfect. Another dream had died—the dream that I had the perfect parents. With that dream went the part of me that was trying to be perfect. There simply wasn't a place in this world for her. She actually should have been relieved of her duties long ago.

The late Michael Yaconelli in his book *Messy Spirituality* tells the story of a boy named Carl. Carl was the last player at bat when he struck out, ending the baseball game and sealing the loss for his team. Crushed and dejected, he didn't notice that his family filled the empty ball field as the other players and their fans quietly dispersed. His family coaxed him out onto the field to continue the game for him, throwing pitch after pitch until finally his bat made contact with the ball. He made a home run that day. That's how he and his family remembered it. As Michael puts it, "I watched a little boy fall victim to a conspiracy of grace"

(Grand Rapids, MI: Zondervan, 2002,p 67). I so wanted that. I wanted my family to come around me, my parents to hold me, to understand and offer whatever help I needed to get out of this affair. But I stood on the baseball field alone, head down, and completely deflated.

Friends disappeared like the leaves that slip slowly to the ground in the fall. A once-flourishing list of friends left behind the barren limbs of winter. I have come to understand that they really weren't friends. True friends stick with you. Like my desire for my parents, I wanted friends who could tell me my choices were destructive but love me anyway. I had a few of those. I think their kindness and support are what helped me survive and actually come out of all of this a much more integrated person.

My thoughts turn to Hester Prynne again. She was entirely alone. No one would give her the time of day. No women would invite her over for tea or ask her how she was doing. None would confide in her that they either shared in her sin or at least had thought about it. Nope. She was isolated from her community and isolated from healing in the context of loving relationships. I know she's a fictional character, but part of me wonders, if she were real, how much of herself did she have to dissociate from in order to survive? A person can't go through that unscathed.

I remember one group of friends—the last. There were four of us who gathered together each week to walk. I really enjoyed that time. They seemed to be sharing more and more. I couldn't. I had revealed what was going on to only two people at that time, so there was no way I would break my silence. Suddenly there were no more walks. "No, I can't make it ..." When things were made public to volunteer leaders at the church, no one called. No one checked in. No one ...

Interesting side note: I recently learned from one of these women that when they asked me to meet with them, they all knew about my affair. They were meeting with me because they thought they could save my marriage, but they never mentioned it. They never said anything to me about my affair or my marriage. I had no idea they knew. What were they doing? I don't get it … I guess it's easy to be on this side of the events and question them. Perhaps they didn't even know what to say.

I have learned in the last few years that people like me are threatening. Because of my scarlet letter, I might "rub off" on someone and they might follow in my footsteps. Or maybe my affair came just too close to their skeletons. To keep the door firmly closed and the past hidden away, distance from any threat to revealing the truth must be maintained. It sort of makes sense to me. I have compassion for those who operate that way, but I know it's so not helpful to anyone. It's our secrecy that creates distance from one another and solidifies the pain we hold so close.

People like me also push people away. We close down doors in our heart and view things from a perspective that sees almost anyone who speaks truth into our lives as an enemy. For me, the truth had to be bathed in lots of grace so that I wouldn't run away from the giver of truth. Like a trapped animal biting her rescuer, I know I refused help from some who tried to set my feet on a better path.

After I quit my job, I felt lost. I didn't know what to do. Part of me wanted to work on things with my husband, and part of me didn't. We went to counseling for a few sessions. I wasn't being sincere. It's basically impossible to heal a broken relationship when part of you wants to stay with the cause of the breaking. It's also impossible when you're not being honest. I still maintained that my affair was emotional. To hold back on confessing the physical aspect of the relationship was like getting dressed and not putting on pants. You can't walk out the door without being fully dressed. Half naked or half dressed is still just half. Counseling with an unwilling individual is a waste of time and money. I was going through the motions to appear as though I was working on things, but I wasn't.

About fifteen months after I quit my job, in the winter of 2005, John finally set an ultimatum. He said I had to choose between being faithful to him and leaving. I hated on one hand that it had come down to this, and on the other, there was relief that he was cutting me loose. It's a hard process to get to the place where you are willing to hear in plain language that the person you thought you were going to spend the rest of your life with is choosing to walk away. John put up with a lot from me. I think he was hanging on, believing I would somehow come back to him, and hoping that I would return to sanity and stop the craziness. I didn't. I never asked him if he was surprised by my answer. Was he expecting me to say that I didn't want to lose him or us and that I could never leave? The words, "I guess I'll have to leave, then," exited my mouth. I heard them, though they seemed distant, as though they came out of some other woman's mouth. Did I just say that? Did I really mean it? In that moment, yes and yes.

The experience didn't feel as emotional as I thought it might. We casually discussed the fact that our daughter was getting ready to start a two-week hospital stay at Children's Hospital and it might be best for everyone if I waited until after she came home. Her stays required both of us participating in either caring for the two kids at home or sitting with her. Divide and conquer. I did not move out of our room at that point. We just coexisted like roommates. How hard was that for John? What was it like to go to sleep next to a woman who had stated she was done? I could not have done that. It would have been far too painful if

I had been in his shoes. Or was it that our marriage and hearts were so separated, so resigned by that point that there was no life left—that even though the words had been spoken, the belief was already there?

We entered the world of separation and all the legal proceedings involved in the dissolution of marriage. I left our home in February of 2005, and on my fortieth birthday in December, our divorce was final. It was not a day of celebration—just a sober acceptance that my dream of having the perfect little family had died and I pulled the plug.

A lot of dreams died in the wake of my affair. I'd like to tell you that life today is better than ever and we are all fine. I do not believe that is the case. Although we are all well into our healing, the pain of the end of so many dreams for so many people is not fine. It could have been avoided. For all that is my responsibility, I missed the mark, and I am indescribably sorry. There is good in my life now, I do have dreams and plans, but they exist within the slight shadow of my past. The consequences of my choices will linger most likely for the rest of my life. Have good things come of all of this? Yes, but at a price.

I am incapable of doing the right thing. I will never be perfect. That dream is dead too. With its death has been the birth of the true me, the flawed me, the me I love, the me who must cling tightly to God. It is the me I am finally at peace with; well, most of the time.

Chapter 6

Failed Escape Attempts

HROUGHOUT MY AFFAIR, ESPECIALLY WHILE I was still married to John, I wrestled with what I was doing but the challenge of withholding the powerful desire for Ethan from myself was intense. It weighed on my heart and my mind. At times it seemed to consume all of me. I so desperately wanted someone to come and rescue me. If there had been a rehab center for relationship addictions, I would have checked myself in. I tried periodically to walk away on my own. It was not an easy battle to fight, and without the help of others, I believe it's impossible. I tell my clients to make certain they have a team of people on whom they can rely to reel them back in when the temptations are strong … and they will be. Just because we want to turn away from something doesn't mean we will. We might even see and experience the destructive side effects of our given addiction but at times find ourselves unable to stay away. I was there.

It happened many times. It was as though I suddenly dropped into myself and realized the full magnitude of what I was doing, knowing that it was wrong, destructive, and deceitful. I would have a wave of energy surge through my body, mind, and heart. I would perceive a sudden strength. In that moment, I knew I needed to walk away from Ethan. If he and I crossed paths, I would be cold toward him. Sometimes I would come right out and tell him that what we were doing was wrong and I was done. He would look at me pathetically. He would tell me, "Fine, go back to your flat-line relationship with your husband." He would be cold toward me as well. I would think I had said something terribly wrong. I would begin to regret thinking I could just walk away from Ethan. This happened repeatedly. The cycle got worse the deeper I got involved with Ethan.

Once, a few months after we immersed ourselves in a full-on physical affair, I rose to the surface and realized the gravity of what I was doing. Ethan and I met for lunch that day, not in our own town but one about a half an hour away. It was still risky, but since we had worked together, it wasn't unusual if someone were to see us. Somewhere in the course of our conversation, I told him that I could not continue our relationship. It was a crisp, cold winter day. We were nearing Christmas, one of Ethan's favorite times of the year. He had just informed me that his wife and kids would be gone for a few days. He painted a beautiful, romantic picture of the two of us sipping hot spiced apple cider, sitting in front of the crackling fire, and enjoying the sensation of simply being near one another. It sounded great, but my stomach churned. No, *no!* I could not do this anymore. My no's were executed with the intensity of a sledge hammer. There was not a gentle easing into what I wanted to say, just *no!* On this occasion, my words were as crisp and cold as the day.

Ethan looked sincerely wounded. Here he was sharing his desire to connect and I was dropping the blade of a guillotine on his heart. The decision came out of nowhere. In a situation like this, I did not need to worry about how I hurt Ethan. Really, this isn't a circumstance where I would want to repair the relationship so we could remain friends. No, it's not a good idea to be friends with your affair partner. Not only is it not a good idea, it's also incredibly dangerous! But I felt bad anyway. That bad feeling, the one of being mean, prompted me to then try to repair things with Ethan. For the first several times, he would welcome me back. There would be some sort of penance to pay, but eventually he would trust me again.

After I went home and told my parents about my affair and the fragile state of my marriage, I had another experience of full awareness. I so desperately wanted things to go back to the way they had been before my affair. I called Ethan and told him that I no longer wanted any contact with him. Again, he was stunned by my words, which seemed to come out of the blue. He didn't say much. It was a brief conversation, and then I hung up. It could all have ended right there. This book would have an entirely different tone. My children would be secure, with all of us in the same home. Perhaps my marriage would be better than it ever had before. Perhaps not.

I gave the separation from my affair all I had. I told my husband what I was doing but still hadn't come completely clean with him. I spent two days alone in the mountains at a dumpy motel with a tranquil setting immersing myself in wisdom from Beth Moore through videotapes. After returning home, I experienced an amazing transformation in my heart.

The following are journal entries from this particular time of trying to break away from Ethan, as usual, alone.

August 13, 2004—A Friday

I can't explain this, but God transformed my heart today. He gave me a love for my husband. He gave me hope for my and our future. He gave me back my life! There's so much about this that I don't understand, just like the question, how can God forgive me for all I have done and allow me to be His child *yet* ask nothing from me as payment, only a contrite and trusting heart?

My thoughts toward Ethan are still there—though waning. The desire to call him is dissipating and getting easier to deal with. I still, however, must rely completely on God's strength to prevent me from giving in. I must remind myself of John's strengths and remove my expectations of his weaknesses. I can do all of this only by the grace and through the strength of God. I'm taking this one step at a time! I feel so free. A tremendous weight has been lifted—one I thought would never go away! Thank You, Father!

You, Lord, are my Father. You are my first love. I turn to you to fill my *huge* heart. There is so much I desire, and I ask you to fill those: that I would find my wholeness in You; that I would feel complete in You; and that I would feel beautiful, lovely, in You. I pray that I would feel important in You and that I would feel successful in You. I pray that I would feel connected to You, and out of that, I would then be able to flow Your love and fulfilling nature toward my husband, children, and anyone else You put in my path. Thank You, Father. I do not deserve Your love, but oh how I am thankful that You lavish me with it!

8/24/04—A Bit about My Journey

Friday August 13—I've had a major heart change causing me to desire to love my husband, to hug him, kiss him, and tell him I love him. I can't figure out where this is coming from, but I know it's right.

Saturday August 14—John and I talked. I explained what's happened *and* that I am fragile—taking this a step at a time, recognizing I could easily fail.

Tuesday August 17—I told Ethan what was going on. In the past week I have wanted to call—sometimes to find out how he was doing, sometimes to tell him how I'm doing. No contact is best, so I'm refraining. It's a huge fight, though, moment by moment. I am sometimes filled with joy and relief, sometimes grief, sometimes anger, sometimes peace. I'm running the entire spectrum of emotions.

9/2/04

Ahhhhh—this has been a *really* hard week, not day, and really not moments. I have *moments* of reprieve, but most of the time I have been on the edge. I so desperately miss Ethan, all facets of him. I'm having a really hard time getting him out of my mind and heart. At times it is unrelenting pain and others, desire. *This* is part of the reason God calls us to remain faithful to our spouse. It's not so much about limiting our pleasure as it is about limiting our pain. I know that *now*. Oh how I wish I had feared God enough to stay away from the fire!

I'm desperate for help. I want someone to enter my life who can speak truth compassionately to me, who will walk *with* me on this journey, *not* push me forward or in the direction he or she wants me to go. ***Help!***

I am in the most difficult battle of my life.

9/3/04

Totally cool day. After I prayed yesterday, I felt the grip loosen. I didn't necessarily feel joy, but I did experience a sense of release. Oh did I need that big time. I couldn't have gone on much longer in that state. I would have called Ethan for sure. I didn't! I am seeing more improvement. I'm getting stronger—thank You, God! Today has been great (not the entire day, but it has built to this moment).

10/20/04

My silence says *a lot!* I've clearly fallen again—by a simple phone call on 9/4/04. I am unbelievably weak! I sure wish I had known this earlier in my life. It would have saved a lot of people a lot of pain! I'm really not going to go far with this new chapter ...

After all the ups and downs of trying to break free from Ethan, I only commented briefly in my journal about how I fell again. I tried several more times to end my relationship with Ethan, but all resulted with us getting back together. I just didn't have the strength to end my addiction to him. I have said it before: I tried to do it completely on my own. Yes, I sought out God's help, but I never reached out to a person to walk through the withdrawal with me. I am convinced that we cannot end destructive cycles on our own. We must walk with at least one other person. Really I think it takes a team of people! That's why organizations like Alcoholics Anonymous and Celebrate Recovery (a biblically based international recovery group that addresses a wide scope of addictions and relationship issues) are so successful. In a beautiful context of both grace and truth, AA and CR incorporate a community to support and encourage one another as participants end their cycle of addiction. Both organizations have created the ideal environment for healing by cultivating an arena where all of who we are can be present, accepted, and encouraged to grow.

Chapter 7

Healing Spaces

FTER ANNA WAS RELEASED FROM THE hospital, I knew my welcome at home was over. In fact, I actually sealed my own eviction. I needed somewhere to live and hopefully heal. My first place of healing was not like anything you might have seen in a movie. It was not like those beautiful, perfectly decorated, Victorian homes set in the country somewhere, scenes of sunlight streaming through the dense and inviting, majestic trees. Or maybe you think of a beach house deserted by the throngs of summer tourists and surrendered to the perfect tranquility of a warm, September sunset. Violins and cellos beckon us to believe that if we could possibly find this mysterious place, we too could experience the deep healing found only in a perfectly placed dwelling. No, my place of healing was a basement bedroom in a dusty home. My temporary room served as the hallway for the teenage boy of my good friends to pass through on his way to the laundry room and bathroom. It was anything but tranquil and perfectly placed!

With all due respect, however, it was my respite. The inhabitants of this very real home provided me with warmth, acceptance, and a reminder that I was going to survive this chapter in my life. I would survive my sentence of the scarlet letter, and life would go on. I didn't accept this truth at the time, but now, looking back, I see that place of healing as the beginning of a five-year journey to deeply soak in the truth that God loves me through and through. He knows of my indiscretions but does not look at me with them in the backdrop. Instead, He sees my beauty, my strengths, my goodness—the parts of me I thought I might never be reconnected with as I was draped with my scarlet letter … the letter of shame.

It was February 2005 when I started living with my friends.

Karen

The spaces that provided healing for me were not at all what I might have envisioned. In addition to my friends' home, I began meeting with another friend of mine, Karen. Karen and I had been friends before my affair. Karen told me later that she had a choice to make. She was friends with both Ethan's wife and me. One day she sensed she was supposed to spend more time with me, which inevitably meant her friendship with Ethan's wife would come to an end. These are the realities of broken relationships. It really isn't possible to be friends with everyone involved. Even now, six years after my divorce, all of our friends made a choice to side with either my ex-husband or me. Very few people chose my side. Something about that scarlet letter makes being my friend shameful. It hurts, but I get it. These are the natural consequences of my actions.

My friendship with Karen started years earlier. We hadn't spent a lot of time together before my affair, but we knew each other in a casual sense. We got together a few times to play cards, and she made the best peanut butter marshmallow goodies at Christmastime (and still does ... can't wait for December!). As Karen and I began meeting every other week to walk, my heart began to heal. It was a small change, but it was a beginning. When the weather got too cold to walk, we started meeting at a coffee shop. At first we just spent time talking. Then we began doing studies together of various books or people in the Bible. We continue to meet every other week, spending a large chunk of our two hours together just talking. For both of us it's new to be in an ongoing relationship. I have three other friends with whom I get together infrequently. When we get together, it's great. We catch up on the happenings of the past few months, laugh a lot, cry sometimes, and then say good-bye until the next time we manage to squeeze one another into our busy calendars. But those friendships are not the same as the one I have with Karen. She and I are committed to growing, and we hold one another accountable. I treasure our friendship.

I'm not a very good friend. People who isolate themselves don't tend to be good friends. We are fine doing life on our own. Well, that's what I used to think. I now realize that isolating myself got me into a pile of trouble. With Karen, I have chosen to abide by the law of full disclosure.

A Victorian Village

I stayed at my friends' house for about two months. I needed a space of my own so I would feel comfortable having my kids with me. I found a furnished carriage house over the garage of a beautiful, Victorian home. It was a soothing neighborhood with brightly colored homes, lush landscaping, and an aura that all was right in the world. My reality was so far from that, and I needed the salve. My kids started staying with me a few days each week. It was good to be together. When I first moved out of

John's house, I would get up early and go "home" to be with the kids while they got ready for school. They were still fairly young (thirteen, eleven, and eight) to be left at home in the morning, and John was an exercise enthusiast, leaving the house around 5:30 every morning to work out. Not wanting to disrupt his life more than I already had, I suggested I stay with the kids in the morning as well as after school until he got home. It worked out until my ex-husband didn't want me around the house anymore, which was understandable. It was time for each of us to start living life completely independent of the other.

I tried to make my time with the kids special. We would make root beer floats, watch movies, go shopping, head out for walks in our picturesque neighborhood, or play at the playground. I did my best to be available to the kids emotionally, but I'm sure my heart and mind were often distant. One morning, as I sat on the toilet noticing the details of the bathroom, the realization that this was actually my life, not a dream, whiplashed into my head. *Really? This is my life?* I thought of all I had done and why I was living in this tiny studio apartment and was overcome with grief. I took a deep breath and had to move on. I had to get it together for my kids.

After a few months in the carriage house, I found a house in the same neighborhood to rent. It was a New Orleans style home with wrought iron porches on two levels of the front of the house. The inside felt like a Victorian home with separate areas for the kitchen, dining and living rooms, unlike the wide open floor plans of the more modern homes of today. I loved sitting on the front porch on the second floor off my bedroom or on the flagstone patio in the back of the house, listening to the birds and gentle sounds of the warmer months. I felt almost normal. It was a respite from the craziness in my world.

I was now attending graduate school for a master's degree in counseling and working part-time. I had taken out a student loan and received some money from my family's business which helped subsidize my meager part-time wages. I didn't request money from John at that time. I paid for everything the moment I left the house. It seemed the right thing to do. I still carried guilt for having left my husband, but I didn't feel bad enough to stay in the marriage. I wonder what would have happened if the money wasn't there. Would I have gone back to my husband having felt the full effects of life on my own? Would that have been for the right reason? There are many questions left unanswered.

I wasn't the only one in need of healing spaces, my kids were surviving all that was going on but they were not happy about it. The girls especially let me know of their disapproval of me. My daughter, Grace said one day that she was ashamed of me. That statement really stung. At the time, I resented that she felt that way. I started seeing my story expressed in her writing at school. As I came across one assignment I felt the blood rush to my cheeks:

the phone cuts my sleep
threatening my peaceful lull
"Unknown Caller" blinking in orange
but she knows
and her hands of treason snatch it up
and her words of sin fly to a place where her suburban life is
    forgotten
where the other man can soothe her
where her children dissolve
and I'm like a turtle
pulling into a shell my emotions bounce and echo
slithering out of the situation while

red clouds my vision
outside where baby chick flakes of snow soften
the cold refreshes my mind
sending goose bumps erupting on my arm
emotions are dampened and the
silence crashes upon you in waves of self-realization

Shame like a heavy stone weighed on my heart. I knew I couldn't shut down her expression—it was part of her healing—but I longed to pretend this was just fiction and had nothing to do with me. I wanted to hang my head, avoiding eye contact at the school. I was certain that all the teachers knew what I had done and were making their judgments about me.

One morning, Paul told me he was sick. When I asked him what was bothering him, he told me he couldn't go to school and that he would rather die. "But you're only ten! How can you want to die? What can possibly be that bad?" I asked.

I didn't get a full answer, but I knew enough not to make him go to school that day. I let him stay at home and we spent some time together. I told him I wouldn't tell his sisters why. We would just call it a mental health day. I held to that promise until he gave me permission to write it in this book. I don't know for sure if his mental health day was related to my affair and the separation of his family, but I believe that it was.

Anna displayed the most anger of the three kids. She was now fourteen. My affair with Ethan had changed some of my attitudes and actions. Anna could see right through me. She said I acted like I was "all cool" telling her that I knew what it was like to be a teenager. Later, she told me that I couldn't possibly know what it was like to be a teenager whose mother had an affair and ripped apart a family, her family. She was convinced that I had crossed the physical boundary with Ethan and she was right, though I never admitted to that. I lost her respect as a human being and more importantly as a parent. In order to live with myself, I had become adept at justifying my actions. I held to my affair being only emotional and that even after I was divorced, I still didn't cross physical boundaries with Ethan. A fourteen-year-old was able to see right through my lies.

Out of Anna's anger, she was cruel and disrespectful to me, understandably so. At the time, the part of me that knew I was wrong would seep in and cower to whatever Anna said. The part that justified my relationship with Ethan would get defensive. It was an unpleasant situation for both of us and I didn't know how to handle my circumstances or her emotions. At some point Ethan told me I needed to stand up to Anna. He was right. Although Anna was justified in her lack of respect toward me, I was still her mother. Supported by Ethan's urging, I spoke with John and asked if Anna could live with him entirely. He seemed eager to have full custody of at least one of our children. I then let Anna know if she wanted to stay with me, she was going to have to be kind. She didn't have to like me or my decisions, but she had to show common courtesies. She decided to stay. She didn't really want to have me out of her life; she just needed an outlet for her anger. That's not something I realized at the time. I'm sure there are residual effects lingering today.

The Little Church

I remember thinking periodically throughout the years following my affair that I was fine. I felt healed. The most important things in my life had been amputated, and I was doing great! It was in moments like those I spent on the hard dark wood pews of a tiny local church that I realized I still had a long way to go. I can't quite put my finger on it, but there was something about that place, beyond the musty smell of age-old wood, Bibles, hymnals, and people, that enveloped me with warmth, acceptance, and safety.

I knew I felt safe because I bawled my eyes out during almost every service.

It was a small church. Maybe fifty people attended at any given service. It was so different from the throngs of people who attended my previous church. At this present moment, I am again attending a large church where I get lost in a sea of people. There's comfort in that at times, but the family feel of a small church is absent. It was that sense of family, being brought in, that prompted me to continue attending the little church in 2005-2006.

I don't remember the messages. They were powerful, and the brought-out-of-retirement pastor spoke with passion and wisdom born from many years walking on this earth. His voice was deep and full, the kind that beckons attention, but sprinkled with compassion and tenderness, like cinnamon on toast. I often wonder what those faithful attendees thought of me, the single woman who usually sat quietly in the back row crying throughout the service. I wondered if they were curious about my story. Who is she? Why is she here? Why does she keep to herself? Maybe they knew the answer. They had all been walking this earth for quite some time. My guess is they knew I carried a heavy load, and when I was ready, I would let them in on it. No one pressured me to engage any more than I felt safe to. No one looked disdainfully at me, and I knew they cared … in their own way, they cared.

God used that tiny aging church with the larger-than-life pastor in my healing process. I could sit anonymously but noticed and pour out my soul through tears to God. He used the songs, the message, and the people to draw out some of the painful barbs that remained in my heart.

I think I attended that church for about a year. I only went every other weekend when my kids weren't with me. They hated the tiny church. They thought it was old and boring. They couldn't see past the aging décor and musty pews to discover the warmth and tenderness somehow present there. I get it. My kids weren't dealing with the same pain I was mired in. While each was affected by my affair and the divorce, their capacity to process it was quite different from mine.

A weekend at the Jersey Shore

I shared an apartment with three friends during my junior and senior years at Bucknell. After graduation, we remained friends. We attended one another's weddings, sent gifts for new babies and exchanged Christmas cards. Our contact wasn't constant but we stayed in touch over the years. At some point during my affair, I filled them in with what was going on. They knew about my affair and dissolved marriage and loved me anyway.

The four of us had not gathered together since our 10 year reunion in 1998. We decided to convene one summer weekend in Ocean City, New Jersey. When the four of us reunited, I filled them in even more. Unlike some of my family members, these three women held me emotionally. We didn't and still don't communicate frequently, but I know that they have my back. If I need them to be there for me, they will be. They were there for me when I was at a very lonely place in my life. I was still involved with Ethan at the time and each was willing to accept me despite all I had done. It was also a relief that the weekend wasn't spent entirely on me. We all shared our challenges and dreams. I enjoyed the respite from my life back in Colorado.

Chapter 8

Doing My Work

I USED TO HAVE THIS UNRELENTING DESIRE inside of me. I wanted something different than what I had. When I was young and dependent on my parents, I wanted to be living on my own. When I was living on my own, I wanted to be married. When I was married, I wanted children. When I had children and a husband, I wanted purpose. When I had a van, I wanted one with power windows and locks. When I was out and about, I wanted to be wearing newer, better, more trendy clothing. I wanted to look like the totally put together women I saw in magazines. I wanted bigger boobs, better hair, perfect porcelain skin … the list goes on. I don't recall a time until recently when I was content.

I would read stories in *People* and think to myself, *I wish I had the life I read about—people jet setting all over the world, living in the spotlight, having lots of money, and being important.* I was caught up in a bit of a fantasy world, and somehow my relationship with

Ethan had been written into the script. Even as I write this, I'm seriously thinking, *Really?* Yeah, really. I had drifted so far off the path of all that is real—like my children and my husband, Ethan's family, the church—that I found myself in a clearing that seemed exactly what I needed but contained none of what was truly meaningful in my life. Yes, there was good in my relationship with Ethan, but having a committed relationship with him was a fantasy that was never going to happen. I allowed it into my reality, and that is a dangerous journey to take.

When my affair with Ethan was in full swing, I remember thinking he just might be my ticket to achieving all the "more" I wanted. He pushed me and challenged me to be all that I could. I resented this at first because with it came a message that said, "Achieve or I will realize you are not the woman I thought you were." I felt a pressure to keep him interested in me. This motivation propelled me to really go for it. I worked long, tireless hours on my responsibilities, taking each with utmost seriousness. I can remember the feeling of adrenaline surging throughout my body as I attempted to make the impossible possible. I knew if I didn't, Ethan would ream me for my failure. The reward from Ethan was never in the attempt but always found in the finished product.

Ethan had been taught by his dad that there are only winners and losers. Second place is just the first loser. In other words, either win or go home. There is nothing to be proud of in second place. I had always thought that one should do their best and leave that on the field. If your best is second place, be proud of all the work you put in to get there. This clashed significantly with Ethan's "win or go home" philosophy. Being sucked into my fantasy and blinded to reality, I bought into his thinking. There was a part of me that would be so hurt by Ethan's belittling and demeaning remarks about my "failures." As that wounded part of me sat in a heap drowning in her own tears, another part would say, "Hey! Rise to the occasion. Prove to him that you are a winner. Prove to him that you can be everything he thought you could and more." This thinking propelled me to begin one of the greatest gifts my scarlet letter brought to me: I began to work on myself.

I had not thought very highly of the counseling or coaching professions up to this point in my life. It's ironic considering I am now a Licensed Professional Counselor! Even my bachelor's degree is in psychology. I thought about going on for my master's after college to be a counselor but was tired of being a student. I'm so thankful for that decision. I saved many clients from myself by putting that degree off! It wasn't until I experienced the hardships of life and the shame of the scarlet letter that I became soft enough to be able to sit across from a client and understand his or her pain and the difficulty of moving through it, no matter the depth or the cause.

Ethan had been working with a coach for a few years and recommended I do the same. You know the phrase "Be like Mike?" Well, I thought to impress Ethan, I would work with a coach. Now I sincerely wanted to do my work, but I never would have done this on my own. The drive to please and exceed Ethan's expectations of me was intoxicating and highly motivating.

Shortly after John had given me the ultimatum to choose my marriage or move out, Anna was in Children's Hospital for one of her "tune-ups." These hospital visits are a byproduct we deal with due to her cystic fibrosis. I say "we," but at this point it really is "she" because she is the one who must endure daily respiratory treatments, antibiotics, handfuls of pills, g-tube feedings, blood sugar checking, insulin injections, and multiple-week hospital stays. It's a sinister disease.

I knew that as soon as Anna went home from the hospital, my husband expected me to move out. I wanted to figure out how I had gotten to this place in my life. One day while I was staying at the hospital with Anna, I stepped out into the hall and called Ethan's coach. I explained my situation and wondered if he could help me. Ideally, to really be like Ethan, I would work with his coach. But that was not the answer I got. He gave me a few phone numbers of female coaches he thought would be good for me. He mentioned an approach called Shadow Work and directed me to a website to check it out.

While sitting in Anna's hospital room, I began my first endeavor into the world of Shadow Work. I learned that Shadow Work is a Jungian psychodrama approach to working on childhood issues and how they present themselves in present-day problems. It was unlike anything I had ever done in my life. It sounded a bit far out to me, but if Ethan had done something like this, then by golly so could I. I called the first woman on my list, Alyce Barry. She is the sister of the man who established Shadow Work. I figured she must be good.

My first meeting with Alyce was in a restaurant. The moment I met her, I knew I was going to be in good hands. She was genuine, gentle, and kind. She listened intently without judgment as I poured out my story to her. It felt good to come so clean with someone real and not my journal. I had kept so much to myself that to pour out my soul to another person was part of the beginning of moving forward in my life. Alyce was open to working with me and believed she could help. I experienced healing in her presence, and I knew she was the right person for me. I had no idea what I was getting into!

Our first Shadow Work session took place at her house. Alyce lived about a thirty minute drive into the mountains in a small home with beautiful views. I sat at her table drinking tea as I answered her question about what I wanted from our session. We had scheduled a few hours for our session, which is typical for Shadow Work, and I wondered if I could possibly fill the time. Surprisingly, it took the first hour just to tell her what I wanted, which was to know how I had gotten to this place in my life: having an affair, tanking my marriage, and walking away from an intact family.

In the course of a few separate sessions, I discovered so much freedom. I came to understand that I had grown up in an oppressed system. This led to squelching so much of my true self so that I could fit into the mold my parents had set for me. I mentioned to Alyce my snapshot memory of my dad spanking my older sister. We explored that piece further.

Something happened to me that day. I believe that, as a child, I put the very real but disobedient parts of me into a box of sorts. It was something I could control. I put them away. I said no to them. I told them, "It is not safe for you to come out. If you do, I will suffer severe pain." I have never liked pain; whether emotional or physical, it doesn't matter. I haven't wanted to hurt. You might think that's not unusual, and you're right, but I took it to such an extreme that even as an adult, I was bound and determined to protect my first child from it. I never wanted her to have to experience sadness. I wanted to pick her up and meet her needs before she had to feel them. ***Dangerous!*** We cannot grow without pain, and we are not truly living without the existence of sadness and hurt. If we try to cut out the bad parts of ourselves or life, we have to cut out good stuff too. (It's ironic that Anna was diagnosed with cystic fibrosis at four weeks old, beginning an entirely different realm of pain and discomfort that was completely out of my control.)

My very wise four-year-old self did what she had to do to protect me. It wasn't safe in my home to be disobedient—to be real.

At four, one can only understand so much, but I am proud of the strong decision I was capable of making then. The method worked for me. I can remember just once getting a spanking. It had something to do with laughing and not cleaning our rooms. I don't remember my dad spanking anyone very often. It wasn't like I lived in an intensely physically abusive home, but it is amazing how just one action can have devastating ripple effects—and it wasn't even me who received the direct blow.

Shadow Work was my first introduction to the healing world. I spent a few years working with Alyce. We would spend three or four hours "doing a piece of work" on a particular issue I was dealing with, and then I would be on my own for a few months, integrating the parts of me that I was reconnecting with—the parts I had shut away.

During the time that I was working with Alyce, I started a graduate program in counseling. One of my classmates told me about EMDR (eye movement desensitization and reprocessing). There was a training session I could go to as a student and get a reduced rate. Since I knew I was going to need many tools in my tool belt to be an effective counselor, I signed up. I knew very little about this method of dealing with traumatic information. I have since learned that it is a very effective way to help clients work through tough experiences. EMDR is useful in processing trauma that we associate with the "big stuff" like physical and sexual abuse. It is also powerful in helping individuals move through experiences that, while not so tragic in definition, had powerfully negative effects on us, like my witnessing my sister's spanking. Even in situations of teasing, where we might think it isn't all that traumatic when compared to a child who was sexually abused, the teasing can have devastating, paralyzing, or emotionally damaging effects that linger into adulthood.

EMDR works with the natural processing mechanisms of the brain. Research has shown that we process information when we are asleep in the Rapid Eye Movement (REM) phase. The brain is put into REM state by the rhythmic right left stimulation of the movement of the eyes. In EMDR this right left stimulation is created through a few different methods like eyes tracking a light beam or hands holding a device that sends a vibration to the hands alternating on the right and left. The client is fully conscious and chooses the difficult information to be processed. With the guidance of a trained counselor, the client is then able to process tough information that had been stuck because the brain was overwhelmed by the experience and didn't deal with it.

So I entered the world of EMDR. Part of my training involved actually being a client. What better way to know how to utilize EMDR than to sit in the chair of the one needing the work? I thought I had worked through all my issues; I know, that is such a cocky statement. I have reached a much more humble state in my healing. I now know I will be on this journey for the rest of my life. Never will I "arrive." In fact, the more I learn, the more I realize how much help I need. Since I had to have something to work on, I spent some time thinking about what that might be. The picture that kept popping into my head was the snapshot of my sister's spanking, so that's what I chose.

I sat across from my student therapist. She gently asked me what I wanted to work on. I told her that I wanted to look at the part of me that thinks I have to be perfect. She then asked me about my memories of times I thought I had to be perfect. Since it was from a very early memory, she didn't have to ask me to remember the first time I had that experience. She asked me about the negative belief I had about myself based on that memory.

I answered, "That I have to be perfect."

She asked me if I believed I had to be perfect, what negative message did that convey to me using a statement like, "I'm not" or "I can't."

I answered, "I can't make a mistake."

She then asked me what I wanted to believe about myself in that memory, something that began with, "I am or I can."

I answered, "I can be free to be me … all of me."

She asked me how strongly I believed the positive statement. Then she asked me about the memory and the negative statement and my feelings about them. I said it made me sad. She asked if I felt any physical sensations. I answered that I felt a pit in my stomach. She said, "Go with that" and started tapping on my knees with her cupped fingers. She was rhythmically tapping—right side, left side, right side, left side. This was stimulating my brain to go into a state that is associated with processing information. I started processing the scene of my sister and the effect it had on me. My body started tingling all over. Then the tingling started moving into my arms. They felt so heavy, like I was under the effect of some drug, but I was drug free. I let my arms dangle at my sides. I started shaking them like I was shaking out all the icky stuff. Eventually it felt like all the tingling, like Pop Rocks bursting in my arms, drained out of my hands. It seemed as though all that ick started dripping on the floor and then disappeared altogether. There was nothing left.

Now it was time to install the good stuff. The student therapist asked me to look at the mental snapshot of my sister's spanking and say the positive statement. Again, she did the rhythmic tapping, and I saw myself in a yellow twirly dress. You know the kind that little girls wear, and as they spin around, their dress flows out? So there I was, dancing and twirling all around that black-and-white photo in my bright yellow dress. I told my dad that he couldn't keep me in a box, that I was free now, and that it didn't matter if I had bad parts of me. I welcomed them, loved them, and embraced them. It's not OK to act on them, but when I do, they don't have to be shamed. I just need to say, "Oh there you are. Hmmm. What is it that you really want, and is there a healthier way to get it?"

A few years later I learned in a group therapy process connected to the therapeutic approach of Dr. Henry Cloud and Dr. John Townsend, that I needed to bring this four-year-old part of me into relationship with others. I needed to share what my experience has been, to have the tragic effects of my experience validated, and to allow others and myself to speak encouragement to the part of me that isn't perfect.

I said to myself, "It's OK to not be perfect. None of us are perfect. That's why we need a Savior. Christ has done the work of the forgiving; I just need to live freely, enjoy this life, and leave the judging to God. I don't even need to be judging myself. I acknowledge when I do something wrong, seek forgiveness, and move on. There is no need to walk in shame, no need to try to pretend the bad things I do don't exist, and no need to act perfect. I just need to be me."

Through the experience of doing Shadow Work, EMDR, and the Cloud and Townsend approach, I was knitted back together. First I had to undo some of the weaving in my tapestry of life to remove the unhealthy threads or ways of functioning. Then, through good therapy, I was able to find healthy threads to weave into my tapestry that connected and healed the broken parts of me.

If you are interested in any of the methods I mention in this book, find a good therapist who can do this work with you. Shadow Work and EMDR both require specific certifications for their practitioners. This book is not intended to be a replacement for therapy.

Chapter 9

My Turn for Mourning

My mom is scaring me. She is sad because of the whole breaking-up thing. Part of me hates any kind of relationship for that reason, because it's like you're trusting that person to take care of your emotions. It controls you so much that it's scary to think that another person, another greedy, selfish, inconsiderate person just like yourself, has the steering wheel to your happiness. Her life is such a wreck right now, or I guess it has been for years. You think you're one way, usually the perfect way, and then you do something that completely contradicts your beliefs, your entire lifestyle up until that moment. It's like she's lost her footing on her own life. Things are just whirling around you happening, and you can't stop. It's like when you stand on that little island in the middle of the street, waiting for the cars to slow down, but they just keep going, blurs of color and activity.

—My daughter, Grace

Karma or reaping what you sow—the belief that what I do will eventually come back to me—has a heavy hand. I believe that to truly grow as a person, I must experientially understand what I have done to others. I can say that, but to live it out is utterly painful. I know this because I was consumed and then spit out by my own choices.

My relationship with Ethan was struggling. We had continued our relationship for the three years that included my divorce, his release from his duties at church, and his divorce. From the time of his divorce, which happened near the end of 2007, something between us shifted. One day he laid into me about three issues: I wasn't involved as deeply in ministry as he believed I should be; my counseling practice was not as successful as he thought I was capable of achieving; and I wasn't revealing my thoughts and feelings to him. Let's just say I was blindsided. I had spent the entire fall encouraging Ethan as he went through the legal tug of war with his estranged wife. There wasn't room in our conversations for me. Sure, I could have pushed my way in, but it didn't seem appropriate, nor did Ethan seem to have the emotional capacity for me. I do not recall him asking me how I was doing. Conversations quickly launched into the latest drama between him and his soon-to-be ex.

Here I was, not expecting a thank you for supporting him while he experienced one of the worst chapters anyone can travel through, but certainly not expecting a lashing for it. Wow! The slap stung my heart. And that wasn't it. He had more. I just didn't seem to be the woman he thought I was. It didn't matter that before I was even divorced, I had started graduate school, found a place my kids and I could call home, worked part time, and made sure I was available whenever Ethan was in town. None of that mattered.

After my private counseling practice had been open for four months, I had a small but acceptable load of seven clients. I suppose I could have done more to get my name out there. He was right that I wasn't burning the candle at both ends to make my practice flourish. I heard repeatedly from others who had blazed the path before me that it took three years for a practice to become profitable. I wasn't even at the six-month mark. In a county where there's a counselor on nearly every corner, I wasn't concerned, but Ethan was. Something about my drive not measuring up to his expectations of me concerned him.

I have heard it said that the quality in a person that attracts us to them often becomes an annoying wasp sting somewhere down the line. I guess our relationship had reached "somewhere down the line." One of the traits in Ethan that drew me to him initially was that he encouraged me to strive to be my best. I was now seeing clearly just how unhealthy this encouragement was. No, not encouragement—this was belittling, demeaning deprecation, with the goal of motivating change.

The icing on the cake came with the next, "Here's how you're not measuring up." It was in ministry. A few months before, Ethan had been asked by a church to teach one weekend a month to offer relief to the current pastor. Ethan agreed. There was one stipulation: I was not welcome to attend. It is so fascinating to me how expendable some of us are. If you have something to offer, well, we'll just overlook your indiscretions; however, the little wearer of the scarlet letter will have to find somewhere else to go. I was the Conan O'Brien to Ethan's Jay Leno. Some of us simply have to know our place, I guess.

I do not count the decision of the church's elders as a strike against God because I don't believe He would have put His stamp of approval on that decision. It is a strike against man because we like to work situations to our own advantage—myself included at times. I'm not proud of that part of me, but as the karma or reaping philosophies point out, what goes around comes around!

Oh please help me learn this one! Treat others the way you want to be treated. Don't judge others unless you want to be judged by the same measure.

Ethan was relief teaching at a church, and I was just barely getting to the point of walking in a church without being certain that everyone could see the emblazoned A on my chest. Shame was strong, and it kept me from jumping back in. Just going to church was humiliating. Getting involved? No way! I wasn't ready to hear, "We want help but not from people like you." No, that sting was something I just wasn't going to subject myself to. And I got hammered for it. The words, "You're not half the woman I thought you were," exited his mouth. It was another dagger to my soul and a stinging slap to my heart. That was three, and I was done.

I get defensive. It's one of the traits I have worked tirelessly on in therapy. My defensiveness can get in the way of staying in relationship with someone. If I let down my guard enough for you to see who I truly am, the good and the bad, and you point out the bad, I want to shut down and run away. I fear that my bad will repel you from me. I think, *How can anyone see the bad things about me and still love me?* If you identify with this, you are not alone. This is a common issue for a lot of us.

Ethan pointed out some of my bad stuff (or at least what he thought was bad; I still don't see these things from his point of view) and did not add, "*And* I love you." Nope. It was more like, "Hey, you've got this stuff I don't like about you, where you're not measuring up to my expectations, and I'm not so sure I want to stay in." It's real. It was his experience of me. But it wasn't, "Hey, I'm in there with you. I'm going to let you know some of the things I'm thinking about you. They're my opinion. I'm open to discussing them, and I am in with you." Or perhaps, "I love you. I see these things in you that I don't like. Are you willing to work on them?" It's just, "Here they are. I don't like them, and I'm not sure about you."

After seven years of being in a relationship with Ethan, the fire began to die. I soberly imagined our lives together without any rose-colored glasses. You see, as the years wore on, I continued to get healthier. I was looking at things from a very realistic point of view. What I saw was frightening. I noticed a pattern in our relationship that sent me into the counselor's office to get fixed. Something would come up, we would argue, and it would boil down to there being something wrong with me. I didn't want to lose Ethan, so I would go to counseling and "do my work"—again and again. On one hand, it seemed ridiculous that one person held the responsibility for the dysfunction in our relationship. On the other, I invested large quantities of time and money into dealing with my issues. It's ironic that my dad wanted perfection from me as a child and here I was repeating the same relationship. Love for me based on my performance. I thought Ethan was my ticket to growth, and I was discovering that he was the path to a suffocating death.

By this point, I was questioning if I wanted to be tethered to a man who could be so harsh and demanding. I wondered how he might negatively affect my kids. They are not nearly the children he might expect them to be. I have worked hard to encourage them to do and be whatever they want at their pace, not mine. Ethan could destroy my kids, and I wasn't about to let that happen. A few weeks later, I casually informed Ethan that I wasn't certain about my love for him. I told him that my heart was swinging. I wasn't saying we were done. I just felt myself swinging away from him. I was too afraid to say I didn't want to be with him, and saying my heart was swinging seemed safer. I realize now that it must have hit him like a sledgehammer, but at the time, I was emotionally disconnected from the power of my words. He didn't say anything. He didn't seem hurt. Our conversation ended with him giving me a hug and ushering me out the door because he had to go. I took that as, "Everything's OK." Or was it?

Over the next few days, I could tell he was pulling away. He didn't call as often, and our conversations were strained. He never commented on what I had said. I drove with him to one of his speaking engagements, and he never mentioned our conversation, how he felt, or what he thought. At the end of the night, I leaned over to give him a kiss before getting out of his car, and he turned away, mumbling something about sometimes just not wanting a kiss. It was weird.

The next day, Ethan flew to the east coast to meet up with a couple he had known since college. Things were not going well that day. As I sat in church, I realized he and I needed to talk, so I walked out during the service and promptly called him. That phone conversation marked the code blue for our relationship. It was filled with misunderstandings on both sides, poor communication, hurt feelings, and baggage from our pasts creeping in and screwing everything up, not to mention the fact that by now, I was desperately trying to mend things. I was back-pedaling. "It's not that I don't want to be with you; my heart was just feeling a little less love for you. You know that normal sometimes-I'm-in-sometimes-I'm-out feeling?"

This was not true. I was scared. I was afraid to end the relationship I had lost nearly everything for. It is understandable that by the time Ethan returned a few days later, he was done. He insisted on no more communication except through email because I was an unsafe person for him. I didn't communicate for two weeks, and neither did he. I felt fine. I was relieved to be away from the mudslinging and craziness of the last few days.

Then one day it hit me that I was alone. After everything that had happened over the last few years, I had no one. I didn't want to be alone. I had left my marriage because of the hope that one day Ethan and I would be together, and now I was facing what felt like a walk down the gangplank. My addiction was being removed from the shelf. It wasn't about my self-control, knowing that when I was weak I could get a hit. I would never be able to go back to Ethan. Never again would I be able to fill my longing to be in a deeply connected relationship with him, and I freaked out. I told Ethan I was ready for us to work on things … blah, blah, blah. It was crazy grasping to avoid the inevitable pain. What we had was wonderful at times but incredibly unhealthy for both of us. And let's not forget the relationship's origins were completely outside of what God intended for us and our families. I just didn't want to feel utter and complete aloneness. But it was time. Oh was it ever time for me to harvest what I had planted.

I cried myself to unsettled, unsatisfying sleep night after night. When my kids were with me, I kept my crying quiet, but when they weren't, I let the floodgates open wide. I moaned, I screamed, I shouted strings of expletives at Ethan, and then in a heap, I would turn on myself. It was never a pretty scene. In my case, it had to happen, though. I couldn't go on through life never feeling even just a smidge of what my ex-husband and Ethan's ex-wife must have felt. As I look back on the breakup, I realize it was the best gift I could ever have been given. It was the true beginning of me coming back to life, of buds forming deep within the charred landscape of my life. Hope was just underfoot, and it was yearning to be released. The only path I could take to experience it started with my own mourning. And mourn I did.

I don't know if it's necessary to go as deep as I did, but that's where my mourning took me. I fell into a dark and very deep hole. I had never experienced true depression until that moment.

The depression was palpable. I could sink my hands into it, but I couldn't grab it and throw it away. I could see no hope—literally no hope. I had given up my marriage, my job, my reputation, and I thought my future to pursue a relationship with Ethan.

I experienced suicidal thoughts. These were not the "I want to hurt others by hurting myself" suicidal thoughts. They were ones of such deep despair that I couldn't fathom the strength it would take to breathe another breath. My saving grace during this very dark time was that I was so depressed I could not muster the energy to exit out of this life. I remember my darkest moment. I was standing in my laundry room adjacent to the garage. I could only hold onto the door sobbing, grieving with such heaves I could barely stand. As quickly as the thought to end my life flashed across my head, I groaned to God with a desperate plea. I don't remember what my words were or even if there were any. I remember a snatching away of the darkest emotions I have ever experienced. I was not suddenly happy or even content. I was still severely depressed, but I was no longer suicidal. That moment was pivotal for me. As I was balancing precariously on the line of death, God yanked me back to solid ground—still miserable but on solid ground.

My memory is that I cried for about three months. I'm sure I didn't cry for a solid three months. I was working on building my private counseling practice, and I had learned not to bring my personal problems into my sessions. This was a time when compartmentalizing was a useful skill. I tried not to cry around my kids, though I wasn't always successful. One day my daughter and I were walking into a store, and a wave of sadness came over me. I just let the tears roll down my cheeks as I asked the clerk for help finding a product. His confused expression was met with, "The tears? I'm just grieving. My tears have nothing to do with being in this store." I felt really free to just express what was going on inside despite what others might be thinking about me. What a huge leap for a perfectionist!

Another gift came in the form of wisdom from Dr. Henry Cloud and Dr. John Townsend through their Solutions CDs that a friend gave me. They have really practical biblical solutions to our everyday life problems. As I was grieving, one CD was particularly helpful about letting people go. They said to grieve all the parts of the person who doesn't want to be in relationship. So when I would be reminiscing about the good times Ethan and I had, which led to tremendous sadness, I would also remember the not-so-good parts of him and the reasons why we weren't together. It really helped me keep things in perspective. Another useful skill was not to "catastrophize" or create stories. One example of this is the thought that I'll *never* be in a relationship again and I'll die a miserable lonely spinster. All I knew for the moment was that I was not in relationship with anyone *today*. I had no idea what the future held, and I needed to stay in the present with the current facts held in tight reality. I listened to those CDs all the time in the car. I couldn't listen to music. Any kind of music was actually very painful for me. Instead, John and Henry became my car buddies.

I heard again and again on the CDs how important healthy relationships are for living life effectively. I had about three friends nearby at the time, so I called them and got together with them as much as I could. I encountered two more along the way and enlisted their help as well. I began working with a new counselor whose focus was on dealing with why I had hidden parts of myself and allowing those parts to come back online. I started going to a recovery group to address my codependent tendencies. I kept up with studying God's Word and talking to Him, coming face to face with who I am in the context of love. The individual pieces were used by God to mend me together again. I had been ripped apart from head to toe, and God was using all these really good, loving people and situations to weave together again the tapestry of my being. Although I have scars that remind me of my affair, I am more pleased with the healed me because there are parts of me I had hidden that God reinstated when He stitched me up. They aren't always pretty, but they are real. Through this process another wave of healing and a new perspective on being whole and integrated was taking root.

I have come to embrace the concept of God's that we reap what we sow. It was powerfully painful to harvest the crap I had planted when I had an affair, refused to stop, disintegrated my marriage, tore a stable family unit from my children, lied, hid, and failed to keep my fence around my own yard. My actions were entirely self-serving. I had to experience the intense aloneness because that is the result of selfishness. No one wants to be around a self-serving individual.

During the worst part of my depression and "harvest time," I was doing a Beth Moore study on the book of Daniel with my accountability partner, Karen. The book surprisingly is about much more than Daniel's experience in the lions' den. King Nebuchadnezzar was in a haughty state, and God allowed the king's pride to turn him into a wild, psychotic man who lived like an animal in the fields. God allowed the king to be cut down, no longer in leadership of his country and certainly not living with his family. It took some time, but eventually the king fell to his knees and recognized that God is God and he was not. He acknowledged that God's ways are best and turned from living life on his terms to living life on God's terms. God restored him to his throne.

The king's situation hit me like a lawn dart piercing my very soul. I literally dropped onto my face on the floor and sobbed. It was a deep cleansing of the realization of all that I had done.

It could have been overwhelming to feel the full rush of my wrongdoing, but in a prostrate position before God, I was able to feel it, let it go, and place it where it belongs: on the cross. This was a monumental step in my healing process. I love that God says He disciplines those He loves (Hebrews 12:5-11). I believe my realization of the pain my actions caused to myself and others was one of God's ways to discipline me. He didn't rub my nose in my crap, but allowed me to feel the consequences of my choices. He simultaneously offered me the chance to heal and be free, emotionally and spiritually, from the weight of my decisions. To me, that is the beauty of the cross.

Chapter 10

Letting Go

ALTHOUGH I EXPERIENCED AMAZING GRACE AND healing, I didn't always stay there. I'm human, so I would feel really forgiven and free but then a thought or an assumption would enter into my awareness and I would find myself in a recurring place of fear. I was not very good at letting go and walking away. Ethan was, and that helped. We emailed now and then (I always initiated the contact, and he would respond), but I didn't want to completely let him go. I remember back in 2004, I saw a therapist a few times. It was about a year after Aron Ralston, the climber in Utah, cut off his arm in order to save his life after his hand got pinned between a boulder and a rock wall. I thought hard about that. I couldn't cut off this arm. I told her I would rather stay stranded and die than cut off my relationship with Ethan. She could not understand me. I did not go back to her. In 2008, I really wasn't any better at it. Ethan was like food to me. I could go without him for a short time, but then the hunger would come back, fiercely at times.

This time, however, there was nowhere to go with that hunger. Ethan was no longer available to me—not really. Sure, I would text or email periodically, and he would respond, but there was no hint that he wanted anything more to do with me. He was done; he had actually stated those very words. He also included the phrase, "There are just too many cracks in the runway" to attempt another takeoff with me. Why couldn't I just hear that he was done and walk completely away? I was dragging around a dead corpse, hoping it would somehow come back to life. Even though I knew the relationship wasn't good for me, it was what I had given up everything for, and I couldn't see life without it.

I had to move on. I was working with a therapist at this point. First we were working on the parts of me that felt I had to have Ethan in my life. Eventually my therapist introduced the idea that I needed to open myself up to meet other men—not looking for a husband, just getting to know men. What I needed was to realize that Ethan was not the only man out there. But how was I going to achieve this seemingly insurmountable feat? My therapist enjoyed going dancing and was part of a group of people who got together every weekend just to dance. She wasn't looking for a boyfriend, just some fun and interaction. I thought about that but couldn't see myself doing the same. I tried a singles' group at the church for a while. This was good for me, but I felt like everyone was thinking, *She's too old for this group* or *isn't that John's ex-wife?* I turned to another source: the Internet

Internet dating is such a weird way to meet people, but it sure beat trying to pick someone up at the grocery store. I'm not a bar scene girl, my work life consists of clients I cannot date, and I had no other involvement with adults. The computer seemed to be the best place. Besides, my ex-husband met his wife online. How bad could it be?

I was fearful, though. What kind of safety is built in when you meet a total stranger? Normally we meet people because they have some connection with someone we know. When I met John, my friend Rita knew him through a friend of hers. Her friend Bill knew John well and would have steered us away from him if he was bad news. With the Internet, we can get connected with someone nobody in our circle knows. That knowledge sent uncomfortable uneasiness throughout my body. What if the guy was a serial killer? What was there to stop him from using the Internet to hook up with women and then kill them? The site I chose to use required me to answer what seemed like an FBI interrogation. It also cost money. I decided that maybe those two factors would be deterrents to would-be killers out there. Maybe the killers choose methods that required less time and money … maybe.

As my finger hovered over the "accept" button, doubts and fears swirling through my mind like a dizzying fog, my daughter Anna clicked it for me. She was tired of the drama. "Mom, just try it. It worked for Dad." So scary! At first I thought I needed to respond to every guy who showed up as a potential match. I read their profiles and tried to find the good in each one, giving them the benefit of the doubt. For the first few days, the matches trickled in. After about a week, my matches began flooding my inbox. I was overwhelmed by them. I told myself I was going to have to stop playing the nice, people-pleasing girl. I was going to have to step up and show some cahones. So I did. I got pretty savvy at closing matches before anything got started. If someone seemed like a good match, as soon as I realized he wasn't, I ended the connection.

Something inside of me was healing. Just because a man was interested in me and seemed decent didn't mean he was someone I needed to pursue. Growing in my confidence in myself, I was able to say no to men who didn't meet what I wanted. Obviously an Internet "no" is easier than in person, but I was beginning to exercise my preferences.

After about a month of screening various matches, three guys rose to the surface as potentials. I set up three coffee dates to meet them in person. Guy #1 was not what I had met online. I called him shortly after our face to face meeting and told him I had no connection with him. He actually got mad at me. He pointed out that I had an issue and wasn't giving him a chance. This was good for me because it meant I had to know who I was and what I wanted despite what he thought I needed to do. He hung up on me, then called back to scold me. This exchange confirmed that he was not a person I wanted to spend time with. Guy #2 seemed decent in our computer communication but when we switched to talking, he spoke and texted many sexual innuendos. When we met face to face, the sexual overtones were not there but he seemed cocky and acted like our relationship was much further down the road than I thought. It didn't help that I had already met Guy #3 in person and he had scored very high. Guy #2, at that point, simply didn't have a chance. Guy #3, or Mr. Fifty as Anna called him, had my attention.

Mr. Fifty, otherwise known as David, appeared transparent which fascinated me. His manner of pursuing me also drew me toward him. He lived too far away for my parameters. I was busy. My private practice was growing, and my three children were a priority. I wasn't about to spend time driving excessively to meet up with some guy and then get sucked in and have to change everything. David put a "hi" next to his name. This was a prompt to respond. I normally deleted all men who lived too far away. I didn't even check out their profiles. But David's prompt caught my eye, and I couldn't just send him to the trash. I would at least give this guy a chance. So I clicked on his profile. Immediately I liked what I read.

Most of the guys I had encountered were fake. Because I believe in God and try to follow Him, I wanted to meet a guy who was similar. The only men who showed up for me were those who had listed themselves as followers of God as well. Most of their profiles read like a pasty, starched façade (believe me, I would know one if I saw one!). Everything was about God … *everything*. When answering a question identifying five things they couldn't live without, most had a God-related answer for all five. Mine were: the beach, my children, some level of organization and cleanliness, sunglasses, and friendship. My three things I was thankful for were: God's mercy and grace, relationships with family and friends, and modern conveniences

The things that David listed as those he couldn't live without were God, family, and a Notebook-type of relationship. The three things he was thankful for: "God – each morning is new/fresh with the possibility and hope of getting it right; Family/friends – I cherish every day that I can call or be with them; Health/job – I'm so thankful for both realizing that these are the best days of our lives." David's answers seemed insightful and honest. I didn't think he was trying to be someone he's not or presenting an image of himself that was manufactured to impress.

What I wanted in a man was someone who isn't perfect but is aware of his crap and working on it. David fit that better than anyone else. I was also drawn to the statement he made about wanting a "*Notebook*-type of relationship." At this point, we were only communicating via email, and I questioned him about that, wanting to know more. He thought I was questioning if he really knew the movie. He went on to give me one-liners from several movies, illustrating his desire for the kind of relationship a man will do anything to pursue. He got me with that one.

I brought up two issues early on in our communication. I asked him if he believed we are defined by our past and told him about my affair. David kindly responded that by asking him about it and being honest about my affair told him something positive about me. He also mentioned our sins are as far as the east is from the west (Psalm 103:12). In addition, I boldly mentioned that if our relationship worked out, would he be willing to move because I wasn't going anywhere. If his answer had been "no," there was no reason for us to continue our relationship. He said yes.

We met face to face at a Starbuck's not too close to my home. Remember that I was afraid of serial killers. When I first saw David, he stood up and introduced himself. He had been there for at least an hour, not wanting to be late. He bought me a latte, and we sat down. He pulled out several IDs. Without ever hearing my serial killer concerns, David thought I might want to know that he was legit. He works for a government agency and was in the Air National Guard. He had both forms of identification laid out on the table in front of him. I giggled and told him about my fears. He said his intentions were good.

Something about him put me at ease right away. I felt like an equal with him. He had no pretenses or macho attitude that he was trying to defend. He was just this very real, honest man. I have learned since our first encounter that he can't keep a secret from me, and the man he presented to me at Starbuck's is the same man today. We talked without ceasing for about an hour and a half. The conversation just flowed, and suddenly it was time for me to go. As we stood in the parking lot, David gave me a hug. He looked at me and asked if I felt anything. I told him I didn't. I had just met him. What did he expect? I did tell him that I enjoyed meeting him. What I didn't say right then was that I looked forward to seeing him again. I hopped in my car and drove away. I seemed casual, but inside I was thrilled that I could move on.

David pursued me like a gentleman. I loved it. It felt so good to be wanted again. This was also a relationship where I was encouraged to grow with positive motivation. David is not one to use belittling as a form of criticism. I get mad and irritated with him sometimes, and I don't always like him, but he consistently encourages me. That means more to me than almost anything. His encouragement comes out of a desire to love me as unselfishly as he can. The guy has his flaws as do I, but in the areas where I have the greatest needs, he meets them. I am so thankful for him.

A few weeks after our Starbuck's meeting, I invited him to join me in Aspen for the Fourth of July. It was a bold move but intentional. I wanted my family to meet David and tell me what they thought. Yes, some of them were the very people who told me I was going to hell and wasn't cute anymore. Although there are aspects of my parents and siblings that can be incredibly painful, they are still my family. We have talked since then and the "going to hell" comment has been recanted and explained as being misunderstood. I have also regained my "cute" status. The beauty of my family is that we all have our crap and are getting better at loving one another in the midst of it. No matter what, they are my family. I love them and value their opinions.

Although my family found David to be somewhat annoying, they liked him. He has this golden retriever type of personality where he runs from person to person asking repeatedly how he can help them. You kind of want to give him a Xanax. It's endearing eventually as you realize that he really does just want to please, and his ADD makes it nearly impossible for him to sit still sometimes. He finds meaning in his ability to help others. His job sucks life out of him. Giving to others seems to fill him back up.

While in Aspen, David and I had a moment together that proved to be a pivotal point in trusting my heart to him. One night we sat on the floor of my room until 1:00 in the morning quietly talking. Without any light, the room was peaceful, serene. Somehow the conversation turned to my affair and how much I regretted bringing devastation to so many people. I began crying, and David leaned toward me, kissing my tears as they trickled down my cheeks. He whispered what an amazing woman I was to admit the hurt I had caused and humbly desire to make it all right. He caressed me with words of tenderness and kindness. He spoke of his own missteps and awareness that none of us are perfect. He reminded me that my affair does not define me and that he believed God had big plans for me. In that moment of vulnerability, David's words and presence healed some of the very deep wounds in my heart. I felt completely accepted by him. He had every right to end his relationship with me. His first marriage had ended because his wife had an affair. He didn't need to be around another bearer of the scarlet letter. I would have completely understood if he said he couldn't trust a woman who had walked away from a decent marriage for another man. But he didn't. He held me. He accepted all of me and saw the good in me—good I sometimes couldn't see.

Over the course of the next few weeks, David and I spent as much time as we could together. We talked for hours on the phone. He asked one night if we could pray together before ending our call. I thought it was different, but sure, why not. That phone prayer became a tradition we have kept since then. Either on the phone or in person, we do our best to pray together every day.

I knew our relationship was moving fast, but I wasn't entirely ready for how fast. About six weeks after we met, David told me he wanted to spend the rest of his life with me. He's eight years my senior. He said he's been around long enough to know when someone really special comes along. He didn't want to let me go. He made sure I understood he didn't mean that I was something to own, just very special.

David officially proposed to me on August 30, 2008, during a weekend trip to Aspen. It was romantic, heartwarming, and I was completely present to enjoy it for all that it meant. Strangely, within a few weeks of David's proposal, Ethan called, out of the blue. He asked if I would meet him for a walk. He had not talked to me since June ... this was odd. I was standing in a bridal shop trying on wedding dresses with my daughter, Anna. I told him I couldn't talk just then and would call him back in a few hours. I looked at Anna and told her who it was. Both of us thought it was ironic. I didn't know how to tell him about my situation with David, but I knew I had to get it out quickly. When I called him back, I said I couldn't meet with him and that I was getting married. Ethan mumbled something about wanting to go for a walk to talk about some big decisions he was making at the time. Then he said, "Well, I guess that answers my question." That was the end of that ... or was it?

A friend of mine who happens to be good friends with Ethan asked me to meet her and her husband for lunch. The request was completely out of the ordinary. She and I got together periodically for lunch but never with her husband. I asked if this was some kind of intervention. She responded with a sheepish, "Maybe." A few days later, I was sitting across from my friend and her husband. They explained to me that Ethan was very sorry for ending our relationship. He had informed them that he never intended for our separation to be permanent. That was news to me. They were very touched by his pain and wanted to do whatever they could so he would feel better. They wanted me to meet with Ethan.

Are you kidding me? Whoa! They were asking me to meet with them and Ethan to see if we could repair our relationship—for Ethan? Where was this last spring when I was utterly depressed, dealing with the most significant loss of my life—when I didn't want our relationship to end, huh?! I was hurt and angry at the time. Clearly their allegiance was with Ethan. Most of the time that doesn't bother me anymore but every now and then the hurt pops back up.

I called David on my way home from lunch. I poured it all out to him. I told him that my friends wanted me to give Ethan another chance. I expected David to tell me that he didn't want me to meet with Ethan. Instead, I got the last response I ever expected to hear: David encouraged me to go ahead and meet with Ethan. What? No part of me wanted to. I was not curious to see him again, to find out how he was doing, or to hear what he had to say. I had no interest. I was actually perturbed by David's suggestion. I wanted him to protect me from ever seeing Ethan again. Sometimes, David is more balanced than I am. He can see the big picture when I get caught up in the miniscule details. He defended his position that it might be an opportunity for me to either bring complete closure to my Ethan chapter or to reawaken a passion to be with Ethan. David wanted to know that I was certain that my desire for Ethan had permanently ceased.

David had a vested interest in this. Ironically, his ex-wife had been involved in an affair for a significant portion of the thirteen years they were married. She had fallen in love with a man she met at work a few years after their wedding, and David spent the remaining years trying to convince her to stay. He was not the least bit interested in replaying those tapes. I understood completely. I knew my heart for Ethan had dried up and shriveled away, but David didn't know that. I acquiesced.

Ethan and I met for lunch on a perfect sun-filled, blue-sky, warm fall day. I was relaxed as I sat in the sun waiting for him to arrive. I knew my position. My heart, and my mind were my guide, and I was confident that I would not be swayed by Ethan's smooth talking. A shadow passed in front of me. As I opened my eyes, there was Ethan towering above me. I hopped up and said hello. We briefly hugged. Nothing—I felt nothing. There were no butterflies leaping in my belly, no pitter-patter of my heart. All I felt was the familiarity of being around this person but nothing more. I liked it!

After being seated at our table, Ethan proceeded to whip out a list he had compiled. It was his "Big Eleven" reasons for why he wanted to be with me. He explained it was like the Big Ten conference in college sports. At that time, though it was named the Big Ten, there were really eleven teams that belonged to the conference. Each comment stated something heartwarming and specific about the good things I bring to life. Tears welled in my eyes as I was moved by the memories. I took comfort in the awareness that my tender side was present. I was not compartmentalizing to shut Ethan out of my life. I was fully engaged, and I still felt nothing for him. None of his words moved me to desire closeness with him. Our relationship had been broken beyond repair. The passion, the desire, the dependency, and the Technicolor experience were all gone.

A deep sense of satisfaction enveloped me. I had confidence I had not felt until that moment. I didn't need Ethan in my life to be OK. Why had I gotten sucked in to believing that? Why had I gone down such a dark and destructive path to be with him? What happened inside of me that I chose to don the scarlet letter and discard the treasures of my life? I believe I didn't know what I was doing. I believe in many ways, I was framed. I had been duped somewhere along the way by the expert deceiver, and I bought into the lie. Not now. Now I am free—well, at least as much as it depends on this situation. I'm clearly quite gullible.

I drove away from that encounter with contentment. I had peeked around the corner to determine whether I wanted a relationship with Ethan. There would be no "what ifs" down the road. Ethan's parting words to me were something about enjoying my flat-line life with David. Because Ethan was hurting, he chose to fling a barb at me. It didn't stick. In that moment, I realized that the timing of David's entrance into my life could not have been more ideal. My relationship with him showed me how positive and healing a relationship can be. He showed me that men can be kind and that the verbal barbs I had received from Ethan over the years were not acceptable. No part of me wanted Ethan back. How often do we get an experience like that? I was just given the most beautiful gift in the world: freedom!

For seven years I thought I could not live without Ethan. I equated removing him from my life to cutting off an appendage. When Ethan performed the amputation, I thought I was going to die. As time wore on, I healed, looked down, and saw that I actually had all my arms and legs. Nothing I needed had actually been removed. If anything, I was experiencing weightlessness as the heavy burden of my affair and relationship with Ethan were gone. I wasn't going to run to Ethan's side and comfort him. I walked away from him for good. I was free, content, and fully alive. I felt like a graceful swan perfectly gliding along in the water.

Chapter 11

Time for Amends

THE PROCESS OF HEALING REMINDS ME of turbulence when flying. Sometimes I am doing fine, not really thinking too much about my past. This state of being is similar to being lulled by a good book, engaging movie, or "mind candy" magazine when flying. My thoughts aren't focused on the plane or the fact that I'm miles above the earth completely without control of how things are going up in the cockpit. All it takes is one stomach-is-now-in-my-throat drop in altitude to snap me into the reality of where I am. One moment I'm just going about enjoying my life when something slaps me in the face and I reluctantly clutch the scarlet letter emblazoned on my chest. It might be the sight of a long-unseen acquaintance or former ministry partner or even the lines in a movie.

I'm quick to reapply the shame and guilt of my choices. I almost want to scream out to people so everyone will know, "I really screwed up! I know it, and there isn't anything I can do to make things right again. I take full responsibility for my part in things. I am so sorry for my choices, and if I could do it all over again, I would choose wisely. Will you please forgive me? Can we just get on with our lives?"

It's amazing, but just writing those words brings tears to my eyes. I guess that might be what I want: to set the record straight with everyone. I did the best I could by making amends with my ex-husband, Ethan's ex-wife, and the elders of the church. I emailed my ex-husband one day and apologized. I told him I didn't do a good job of respecting him and asked if he would forgive me. He emailed back saying he already had. It was a sweet feeling to read that. About a year later, I called just to tell him how sorry I was, how barely a day goes by when I don't regret what I did and how I treated him. "I'm so sorry …" I was sobbing. It was hard to get the words out between the gut-wrenching tears. With each breath, I did my best to convey to him that my heart and head were fully connected and I was not side-stepping the gravity of my affair or the way I treated him. I wondered if that might have given him a sense of satisfaction: "She's finally feeling what she did. She's finally experiencing a touch of the grief I had to go through when she walked away from me and away from our marriage." Maybe that's what he thought or maybe not.

I wrote Ethan's ex-wife a simple letter. Honestly, what could I say to her? I know I'm not responsible for her ex-husband's choices, but if I had just walked away from the temptation, her life would be quite different, and I would hold no responsibility for her pain. As it is, I know that I played a role in the disintegration of her marriage. I stated that I was sorry for crossing God's boundaries with her husband. I told her that if there was anything I could do to please let me know. I wonder if as she read my letter, she said to herself, "Uh, a little late for this … can you heal my broken heart? Can you give me back all the lost moments to the depression and anguish I felt as my husband left me? Yeah, there's something you can do … go to hell!" Maybe—maybe that's what she thought. I don't know, and I really don't care to find out. I just knew I had to apologize, as feeble and poorly timed as it may have been.

My sin against the church was weighing on my heart as well. How could I apologize to an entire congregation? If you know anything about the Celebrate Recovery approach to healing (similar to AA), then you know Step six is to make amends. But the step is careful to point out that they should only be made as long as the amends don't hurt anyone in the process. It didn't seem possible to bring up an icky part of the church's history now. There did not seem to be an appropriate forum in which to express an apology, so I went to the elders of the church.

It was a Friday morning in June 2008. I remember just a subtle anxiety prior to that day, but the true nerves arrived that morning. It was rather intimidating to go in front of the shepherds and guardians of the church to admit that I had violated their trust in me. Petrified inside, I prayed that God would help me. More than anything, the message I wanted to leave with the elders was that I was sorry for betraying their trust. I had, after all, been given a huge responsibility when I was brought on staff. In addition to the elders' role of protecting the church, it was my role too. As a staff member, that fact had to be first and foremost. Maintaining the integrity of the church starts with the staff. And I had failed. I let them down. I let my teams and volunteers down. I let myself down. It is so painful to realize that.

If I could send a warning to those in leadership, it would be, remember you are being watched. What you say, what you do, and how you do it all represent God and the church to the people around you. Do not step lightly into that role. It is one with tremendous responsibility. Perfection is not the expectation, but sound integrity is. I had not heeded the words of Peter Parker's grandmother in *Spiderman*: "With great power comes great responsibility!" So here I was offering an amends to the church.

The elders showed kindness and care. It felt a bit like I imagine it felt for the adulterous woman when Jesus said to her, "Neither will I condemn you, but go and sin no more" (John 8:11). I imagine Jesus saying those words to her with all the tenderness, kindness, and compassion she needed to truly absorb them and walk away with her head held high, knowing she had just been bathed in God's ultimate forgiveness. I don't know if that's how they felt, but it was my experience, so I'll go with it.

My ex-husband's parents are another entity I sensed needed to hear something from me, or could it be that I believed I wanted to talk to them to say what I thought needed to be said to clear the air. My ex-father-in-law wouldn't even look at me anymore. Though John's parents lived thousands of miles away, they came to visit once or twice a year. Inevitably I would have to stop by the house to pick up the kids and their belongings when it was time for them to be at my house. I dreaded those moments. John's mother worked hard to be kind and I could see the hurt and disappointment in her eyes. John's dad treated me like I had the plague. I remember one time when I entered the house, John's mom looked up at me from the bottom of the stairs, turned around, and headed the other way without saying a word. I said hi to his dad. I think it about killed him to even acknowledge I had spoken to him. He mumbled something and then turned away.

I get it, really I do. It hurt like crazy, but I doubt I would have acted differently. From this side of the table, I would like to say I would be gracious, but maybe in the moment I would forget about my own screw-ups and focus instead on my feelings of betrayal.

John's dad worked in the prison system as a guard and captain for most of his life. I remember having a discussion with him about the controversy around the rehabilitation of criminals. His position was that once a person broke the law, he or she was a criminal for life. He maintained that prison conversions were a façade. We talked about Chuck Colson. As a result of Mr. Colson's involvement in Watergate, he ended up in prison. While in prison, he came to faith in Jesus Christ and was convinced that the best solution for criminals could be found in faith. After serving his time, he started a ministry for prisoners called Prison Fellowship. Through this ministry, he trained volunteers to go into prisons and teach Bible studies. Prison Fellowship International is now the largest Christian-based international organization involved with the criminal justice system.

Chuck Colson's life is the story of a man who did something wrong, paid the penalty for it, and turned his life around. My father-in-law believed that Chuck Colson was just a liar. He maintained that all prisoners who experience some sort of conversion in prison are just doing it to manipulate the system and the people in their lives. He believed that every single one of them is a liar and there is no such thing as a conversion. You are what you are, and you cannot change it. I was now included in that group of people in his eyes, and he detests them all. I think he detests me.

I had an interesting encounter with my ex-husband's family in June 2010 at my oldest daughter's graduation party. My husband, my ex-husband, his wife, and I worked together to throw a party for Anna. I entered the backyard of John's house with handfuls of helium balloons. To my surprise, several of his extended family members and his parents were there. They looked at me with blank stares. No one moved toward me. It was one of those moments when everyone but you seems frozen. It seemed like an eternity passed. Finally, I blurted out, "I'm so sorry. I know I did a really bad thing. I screwed everything up. I wish I could change that, but I can't. Now could someone help me with these balloons?"

I think they were shell-shocked. Apparently some of them didn't even recognize me, but it certainly helped break the ice. For me, I got to say what I wanted. It felt good—embarrassing, but good. At another point during the party, I spoke candidly with John's mom. Again I apologized for what I had done and expressed deep remorse about my inability to change anything. I really don't know if she understood, but at least I got the opportunity to say what I believed needed to be said.

I welcome the opportunities to say what I need and want to say. I don't often get the chance, but when I do, I have no problem speaking candidly and owning my part in my affair and divorce.

Chapter 12

Me Too

If you hide your sins, you will not succeed.
—Proverbs 28:13

ESUS KNOWS WHO WE ARE AND who we will be, and He died
for us anyway. I love the story of Peter. After Peter's brother
Andrew met Jesus, Andrew headed out to find Peter and told
him, "We have found the Messiah" (John 1:40–42). When Jesus
and Peter met, Jesus said to him, "You are Simon son of John"
(John 1:42). The way in which Jesus addressed Peter seemed to say
He knew Peter, though He had just met him. Jesus also knew that
a few years later, Peter would deny having been with or knowing
Him. At the Last Supper, Jesus told Peter (also called Simon),
"Simon, Simon, Satan has asked to sift you as wheat. But I have
prayed for you, Simon, that your faith may not fail. And when you
have turned back, strengthen your brothers" (Luke 22:31–32).

Jesus knew Simon Peter would fall away and would choose to do things his own way even though he had walked with Jesus, shared meals with Jesus, and laughed with Jesus. I get a lot of comfort from Jesus' words to Peter. He spent time with Peter and included him in the exclusive group of the three to whom He revealed Himself at the transfiguration (Luke 9:28). Peter was the first to proclaim his belief in Jesus as the Christ (Mark 8:29). Peter was the only disciple to risk getting out of the boat to walk on water (Matt. 14:29). Peter really went for it and when he fell it was not done gracefully.

I can identify with Peter. He was the one who was willing to step outside of his comfort zone at times, who appeared somewhat arrogant, and who face-planted repeatedly. I don't see myself as a teacher or leader of a movement, but I do see the comparison of a person who deeply loves God, wants to honor and obey Him, is at times willing to do anything for Him, yet at others completely turns her back on Him. What I treasure the most is that Jesus told Peter that He had prayed for him, "that his faith may not fail." I cling to the tenderness of that. Jesus knew what Peter needed most, and He prayed for him. Lord, have you prayed for me, too? I believe He has. I also believe that He wants me to strengthen others.

The journey I have taken of turning my back on God so I could do what I wanted to the 180-degree shift of resting in His arms and His will is not just for my benefit. I once heard the story of Helen Back. Helen found herself on the dark side of a chasm, where she finally decided to confront her issues and deal with them. While on this dark side of the chasm, with the help of God, she experienced healing from the pain and hurt in her life. Later she walked across the chasm to the light side. As she stood on the other side, she looked back across the bridge and saw people who, like herself, were held back from living in the light by their hurts, habits, and hangups. She went back to help them because she knew the way, having been to hell and back herself.

Prior to my affair, I had not experienced what it was like to live on the dark side of the chasm. Remember, I had contained that part of myself. I knew I had sin to deal with, but it never seemed all that pressing or that big of a deal. I loved Jesus, was thankful He died for me, and shed tears at times for His gift, but I didn't know the depth of my depravity. I'm sorry it took an affair to find out, but I'm thankful I know! I now identify deeply with the woman at the well, the adulterous woman, and the woman who washed Jesus' feet with her tears. I have wept authentically at His feet. I have been humbled, recognizing I am powerless to overcome my tendency to do the wrong thing and that it is only by the power of God working in and through me that I am even capable of doing anything that resembles the right thing.

One aspect of my journey that I find intriguing is that when I turned my back on God with regard to my affair, I did not shut God out of my life. I very much clung to Him as I careened out of control. I prayed daily. I sought His help to overcome my addiction to Ethan. I never yielded to Him, though, which explained why the clinging and prayer just never seemed to be enough. I know now that what I was trying to do was overcome things on my own, in isolation. During the part of my affair when it was in full bloom and I was still married, I was in a women's study group. We read and discussed *Waking the Dead*, by John Eldredge. After that, we ironically delved into Beth Moore's *Breaking Free*. The leader of the group knew what was going on with me while we were meeting because an elder had told her.

That must have been a tough situation for her. She never told me to stop, never condemned me. I appreciated that at the time. Now I wonder why she wasn't more aggressive. Maybe she feared a negative reaction from me. Maybe she had never dealt with a situation like this and had no idea what to say. Or perhaps, she was offering a safe place for me to process. Although she knew my situation, she told me that sharing it with the rest of the group was up to me. I was welcome, even if I wasn't completely transparent. That I chose not to be open with the group was part of my downfall. I think if I had, I might have had a fighting chance to end my affair and save my marriage—that is, if they could have handled my honesty. Their response is another unknown. Based on my experience, I don't think the women would have known what to do with me. Regardless of these unanswered thoughts, I had not reached a comfort with transparency in my life. I look back at that lost opportunity, and I realize I just didn't trust them.

I think lack of trust is one of the biggest hindrances to healing. Whether we're dealing with an addiction to drugs, food, shopping, sex, men, or TV, there is so much shame in admitting it. We are all carrying some sort of addiction, but we fear revealing who we really are. We fear because we have seen or experienced the judgment that so often follows. Maybe you confided your truth to someone, and she told your secret to everyone. Perhaps you ventured out to seek help and you were condemned, no longer spoken to, and ignored by the one with whom you took a chance to be real. I hear that response more often than acceptance, support, empathy, and understanding. This is heartbreaking. What we need most at challenging times in our lives is one another, and yet that's the time when we tend to hide. We are so good at compartmentalizing our pain and saying, "I'm fine."

I believe it has something to do with self-preservation. Those with whom we share our dirt are afraid of their own. If they are near someone who is flawed deeply, it brings to the surface their own issues, and they are not willing to go there. They fear it might tear down their own walls and reveal what they are hiding. They fear that they might become known. That is such a scary place. The ridiculousness of it is that the only reason we are afraid to be real is we might be seen, so we perpetuate the cycle.

I love the concept of being in a "me too" community. "You have dirt in your past or present. You know what? Me, too." It's Jesus in the temple square with the adulterous woman. He told those who wanted to stone her, "Go ahead if you have no screw ups in your life" (my paraphrase). Each man present, who had previously been eager to stone this naked and ashamed woman to death, began to drop his stones. One by one they turned away and headed elsewhere. It was clear each was not sinless. Each man became aware of his shortcomings and realized he had no right to stone her, for he too was guilty. Maybe these men hadn't committed adultery (maybe they had), but they recognized they were in the same boat as the woman. In the recounting of this story found in John 8, Jesus knelt down and wrote on the ground. While no one really knows what He was writing, many say He was writing the sins of the men who were eager for justice to be carried out on the adulterous woman. When our sin is clearly in the forefront, it sure makes it difficult to condemn another.

In 2006 a man gunned down several young Amish girls in their schoolhouse. I remember thinking about that incident shortly after it happened and wanting justice for what that man had done. He took away the innocent lives of the girls, devastated their families, and shocked the nation. As I was filled with vengeful anger for what this man had done, I suddenly realized that he and the Amish girls could all be in God's presence at that very moment. He may have murdered them, but he could have been a believer. If so, he was sealed by the offering of Jesus. God tells us in Romans 8:38–39 that nothing can separate us from His love ... not even our actions. This man might have been a believer. *This man might be in the presence of God with the very girls he killed.* Does this hit you like it hit me? I wanted this man to be condemned. My next thought was I, too, deserve to be condemned. What I did is still punishable with death by stoning in some places on this earth. If I want justice for him, then I better be prepared for that same justice to be poured out on me.

We tend to be so quick to dole out justice, but when it comes to our own lives, we want mercy. We want forgiveness. We want the slate to be wiped clean. But we want this only for ourselves, not for others. Perhaps that thought hit the men at the stoning of the adulterous woman square in the heart. "Oh, yeah, I'm not without sin. I should go home."

God tells us that no one is righteous, not even one (Romans 3:10). None of us are worthy enough on our own. Jesus was clear in Matthew 5 when he said if we've thought about something, it's as good as doing it. He leveled the playing field. Come on, who of us has never had an angry thought, a steamy thought, or a twisted thought? I know I'm guilty. Shoot! One good thing about wearing the scarlet letter is that I *know* I'm culpable, and so does everyone else who is aware of the letter A emblazoned on my chest. I have nothing to hide.

Because my sin is known by many, I also find that I am more approachable. For those who have had affairs but have told no one and have gone on to have successful marriages, I have been a safe place to turn. I have learned that I am not alone. It would have been helpful to have known this information before. We really can support one another as we go through life. Rather than being against one another, we can be in each other's court and on the same team. Part of my goal in writing this book was to strip down publicly—to show who I am, what I've done, and the things I am capable of doing. Maybe if I say, "Me too," you might feel a bit more comfortable and accepted enough to reveal the truth about you. If we develop a culture of sharing our icky parts and welcoming the icky parts of others, then perhaps we can put an end to hiding and wallowing in our shame. I know how good it feels to me.

I have attended two Henry Cloud and John Townsend Ultimate Leadership Intensives. One was designed specifically for counselors. Both were powerful weeks where I sat under John and Henry's teaching on their understanding of how God sees humanity, healing, and really going for it in life. An interesting and life-altering component of both intensives was small group counseling. The attendees were divided into groups of about eight people. In our small groups, we spent a few hours each day with a counselor getting the opportunity to work on some of our deep hurts and hang-ups in the context of community. I was willing to be vulnerable and shared the basic information about my affair with this group at our first meeting. I had paid good money to attend the intensives, and I wanted my money's worth.

The first intensive was the Ultimate Leadership Intensive, which I attended in July of 2008. I was in a really good place in terms of my healing after my affair. What I found as I shared with my group was relief. It felt so good to reveal the truth about myself. I was somewhat fearful and definitely felt like I had taken my clothes off in front of everyone, but they did something I wasn't certain my kind could do: they accepted me. There was no condemnation or shame. I felt embraced. I could hear their anger toward Ethan, the leadership, and even my ex-husband about how this sort of thing could be allowed to happen in the context of the church staff. I hadn't gotten to the stage of allowing my anger about the situation to be felt yet, so that surprised me. I still made excuses. "The church staff didn't know what to do. The pastor was in over his head. John was a good man. I should have known better. It was my responsibility." And yes, for my part, it was my responsibility, but I need not take on everyone else's part too.

That's for them to deal with. My team challenged my reasoning, which I needed.

I could also almost hear sighs of relief. I was later told that my revelation made it safer for others to do the same. When one person is willing to drop the pretenses, then it's much easier for others to follow. The same thing happened again when I attended the Counselor's One Week Intensive in April of 2010. This time I had done a great deal of healing from my affair, but I was still hung up by a few tangling strands, and I wanted to work on them. In order to do that, I had to reveal my affair again. As the years roll on, the intensity of the pain of my affair is waning. I sometimes forget the impact my experience can have on others. It stirs up emotion in those who hear about it. The fact that my affair was with a pastor and I was also part of a church staff churns within people, resulting in differing reactions. While I wasn't crying about my affair, my openness once again set the stage for others to say, "Oh, she's willing to strip down to her raw self. I feel safe to let my real self come out too."

There's approachability in the honesty we share about ourselves. The book of Esther begins with, "This is what happened during the time of Xerxes." In Beth Moore's study on Esther, we learn that phrase is used five times in the Bible to introduce a situation that included catastrophe or doom. I think my story could have started with, "This is what happened during the time of Karen." I have catastrophe and doom in my history, some things that happened by my own hand and some done by others, and who knows what lies ahead. I am also aware of the way I used to read the Bible. I would read the accounts of Eve, Samson, Sarah, the Israelites, and David, thinking, *Oh I would never have eaten the fruit of the tree God commanded me not to eat. If God told me not to do it, I wouldn't have. Oh my gosh, Samson was such an idiot for telling Delilah how he could lose his power. I wouldn't have gone after her to begin with. Couldn't he see she was trouble with a capital T? As for Sarah, I would never step ahead of God and do it my way. I would have waited on God* ... No, the reality is I'm a lot like Samson, Eve, Sarah, and the Israelites complaining in the desert after they had been freed from four hundred years of slavery. They chose not to follow God but do things their own way. The story of David with Bathsheba is particularly close to home. There's a sobering piece to this realization because I used to think I'm great, and the truth is, I'm not. "This is what happened in the time of Karen ..."

There's a beautiful redemptive aspect to this awareness: knowing that by yielding to God and submitting to His work and His will in my life, He can do amazing things in me. When I think about the fruit of the spirit in Galatians 5:22–23, I recognize that by God working in me, which requires that I bend my knees before Him, He can give me the capacity to love when it's hard to love. This applies also to exhibiting joy, peace, patience, kindness, goodness, gentleness, and faithfulness when I don't have it. It is the same principle with regard to self-control when my opposing desires are screaming in my face, seemingly impossible to ignore. On my own, I can't exercise those attributes. I can kind of do them when things are going great—some of them. But when things are rough and I can't do them in my own power, it's only going to happen by God working through me. I have seen that. I have experienced glimpses of it, but let me say, it's hard work to bend my knee. My tendency is to stand up taller, puffed up and filled with myself. And then, of course, the puffing up is typically followed by the inevitable crashing down.

I like myself better when I'm yielding. I'm more at ease with my "me too" part. The other part of me that thinks she's got it all together and would have spared humanity the entrance of sin into the world picks up rocks. I think we've all had enough of that.

Chapter 13

Hiding to Revealing

I will also give to each one who wins the victory a
white stone with a new name written on it.
—Revelation 2:17

ONE OF THE SIDE EFFECTS OF living with a secret is a lack
of freedom. While I was steeped in my affair, I had to
be careful about what I said and how I said it. My lying
had become a well-honed craft. It was about survival. I couldn't
bear to share what was really going on because I couldn't stand
the thought of people knowing the truth about me. The fear of
being known for who I really am was powerful. It was powerful
enough to propel me toward deeper separation from everyone
around me. I was a great liar, and I was isolated from those who
could help me. I thought they would hate me. I believed that if
people knew the true me, they would want nothing to do with

me. This belief was validated by my mom's comment, "You're not cute anymore."

A benefit of wearing the scarlet letter is that the façade is now removed. The reality of my actions was in plain view for all to see. OK, so only the people who had been told by the church and gossip mills knew, because my scarlet letter was figurative and not literal. I sometimes wish it was literal ... but only sometimes. I am spared that not all know of my choices and actions. Not everyone is safe. Not everyone will appreciate my transparency. Most of the time I don't mind sharing the truth about my past choices, but there are those moments when I would rather not.

There's freedom in knowing for myself what I am capable of. I no longer think that I will do everything right. I no longer rationalize away contact with dangerous people ... well, dangerous for me. I know that I am susceptible to seeking fulfillment outside my marriage. I know I am usually a heartbeat away from making a decision that could ultimately pull me away from my husband. This is not to say that I am constantly battling the temptation to have sex with other men. It's just that based on my past, I am aware of my tendency. It is this awareness of who I am that has propelled me to create some safeguards for myself.

I now enjoy the fact that at any time, my husband can look at my computer or cell phone history and see zero contact with Ethan. When I joined Facebook, I was in the process of adding a friend when a group of about twelve people showed up on my screen. They were all friends of my friend. Interesting that out of the five hundred or so friends she had, Ethan's picture showed up in that select group of twelve. I sat there and looked at it for a moment, somewhat shocked. I hadn't had any contact with Ethan for over a year, and there he was staring back at me from the computer screen. Part of me was curious. I wanted to check out his Facebook profile and look at a larger picture of him. I even wondered for a brief moment if we should be friends.

Notice that I said "brief moment." As quickly as all those thoughts ran through my head, I knew none of that would be happening. I logged off my Facebook account and walked away. There was a day when I would have thought, *Oh, I can just look. What trouble will that cause? Besides, I love my husband. I have no desire to be in a relationship with Ethan. I'm not doing anything wrong.* For me, all of that is just a temptation I don't even want to sample. I don't want to lie to my husband ever! Within a few days of the Facebook encounter, I met with my accountability partner, Karen. I shared with her what had happened. I knew I had to speak this to her. I had been up front with her throughout my healing process. I wasn't going to stop now! I know that honesty and revealing are keys for me in my growth. It was hiding little truths along the way that got me into very deep, raging waters. I wasn't about to start down that path again. I was still drying out from my last encounter with hiding.

Next came honesty with my husband. Now I would like to tell you that I came right out and told him too, but I didn't. It was easier to share with Karen. Here I was back in that place of "I don't want to hurt my husband." That's the very thinking that ignited my action of withholding information from my first husband. Really, I was doing the same thing again? Oh how stubborn am I? Less than a week later, David and I were driving up to the mountains to visit my family. He asked me if I had any conversations with friends about Ethan recently. I told him yes, twice. The first incident was with my mom, who had encountered a woman at her church who somehow knew of my affair with Ethan, and the second was the Facebook incident. I was so relieved to share this with him. It was hard, don't get me wrong. As I began sharing, the burden of holding onto the knowledge was lifted. I let go of the shame of not telling him first before he asked. I'm just thankful that I was honest. It's about small steps.

One thing I am most grateful for in that interchange with David is that I didn't have to tell him that I clicked on Ethan's picture. I didn't have to say curiosity had gotten me. I know that if that were true, I would have to tell him. I'm so thankful for the work God is doing in my heart to help me not go to the places that are dangerous for me. I would like to tell you that Ethan means nothing to me or that I don't even think about him, but that would not be true. There is something about him and the relationship we shared that goes deep into my soul. However, I have learned that just because we have a deep connection with someone does not mean we are meant to be together. I believe that statement with all of my being. Despite the negatives, I know there was good in my relationship with Ethan. Our context was totally outside of God's will, but the connection was deep and very real. It was not built on simple physical attraction. In fact, I really wasn't attracted to Ethan at first.

Not everything or everyone that crosses our path is meant for us to enjoy. Some of you may think, *Duh, of course!* That's just not the way my mind thinks. I used to believe that if something was going to make me happy or content, that it would be fine to do it. I never took this to the point of doing drugs or things that are illegal, just in the everyday stuff of life. If I wanted chocolate for breakfast, fine. If I wanted to spend a day watching movies, go for it. If I wanted to go to Cancun with my family, even if we shouldn't spend our money on that, I didn't hesitate. I'm figuring out now that restraint can go a long way. It's helpful in fact to say no to some things, if for no other reason than to exercise the no muscle.

In the early spring of 2010, I was part of a team at my church that went overseas on a humanitarian trip. Ethan wanted to partner with the same organization and was planning on attending our debrief meeting we were having four days after our return. When I was told on the day of our debrief that he might be there, I stopped breathing momentarily. I was angry. I had just experienced one of the most powerful events of my life in a third-world country, and Ethan had to get involved. I don't know if he did that to wiggle his way into my life or if he sincerely wanted to be a part of the partnership. Regardless of the reason, I wasn't about to be in a room with him for the first time in over eighteen months at *my* debriefing. I felt so unprotected that he was even invited to this meeting. The organizer knew our story. I was uncertain how to handle the information. Initially I took the people pleaser route and squeaked out a feeble, "Sure, that'll be fine." After a few hours mulling it over, I called the organizer and said I would *not* be OK with Ethan's attendance at our meeting. It wasn't because I would want to start a relationship with him; it was because I do not want him in my life. I said no, and though I felt some guilt, I also felt tremendous relief. No is a very powerful word!

My friend Karen practiced saying no. There was a time when each month she picked something she believed God was asking her to let go of—things like movies, sugar, soda, or shopping. Each time she told me what the no of the month was, I grew enamored with her ability. She had good reasons for why each item's number came up. She tried to justify why that item shouldn't be the one that month but then quickly put down her pride and accepted letting it go for a month. I haven't followed in her footsteps! I listened and thought, *Isn't that cool!* but that's too big a step for me. Really, I don't want to. I have said no to the most tantalizing temptation for me to date. I think I'll just rest with that for awhile.

Chapter 14

Freedom from the Scarlet Letter!

I, even I, am he who blots out your transgressions, for
my own sake, and remembers your sins no more.
—Isaiah 43:25

OK, SO IF GOD DOESN'T REMEMBER my sin, then He
is not holding me in a place of punishment—*I am!*
Wow! He's saying, "I've forgotten it. Now move on!"
Hmmm ... *I'm* keeping myself down. In Hebrews 10:11–18, God
talks about this. In verse 14, He says, "Because by one sacrifice he
has made perfect forever those who are being made holy."

I have already been made perfect or complete. That miraculous
change in me occurred the moment I accepted Christ's sacrifice
for my sin (including my affair!). All my sin (past, present, and
future) has been completely removed. I kind of want to jump
out of my skin right now and shout! This is resonating deeply
with me today. I think I am beginning to understand something

profound here. *Yeah!* God, help me to walk as one who is holy and blameless. I feel light, like I could float, when I let go of living under the intense weight of my sin.

As a result of understanding God's forgiveness of my sin, I am better able to forgive myself. When I torment and chastise myself for the choices I have made, I must keep in the forefront the truth, what God says. He tells me I am forgiven. He tells me He will never act in judgment over my sin (Jeremiah 31:33–34; Hebrews 10:16–17). I believe it is either my own voice or maybe even the voice of our primary enemy that tries to hold me in bondage to my past. God's intention is for me to live without the burden of the shame of my choices. That is the way to freedom … no baggage! Satan wants the opposite for me. As John 10:10 says, Satan came to kill, steal, and destroy. If he can do it by burdening me to the point of intense shame and hiding, then for that time, he has won. But that is not what God intended—not for me and not for anyone. Strip off that scarlet letter! Strip off the letter of shame! Walk in freedom!

That feels so fabulous to read. Maybe for a moment you thought you could do it. Your fingers reached for a loose corner of the letter attached to your chest and then fell with resignation to your lap. I know that experience. It is frustrating to know in your head what is true, but getting it to travel into your heart seems the most challenging.

Here's something I do that helps me in this process: Each time you hear lies about yourself, try to notice that you are hearing them. Begin to pay close attention to your thoughts, emotions, and actions. Notice yourself going about your day. This is called awareness. Most of us don't spend very much time being aware of ourselves. We are the masters of autopilot—just skimming the surface of life without really dipping in. Begin to break the cycle by noticing. Turn off autopilot, and start feeling the controls in your hands. You don't have to do this all the time, every day. Just begin doing it a little bit each day. As you get the hang of it, you will find you want to do it more and more. If feeling gets too uncomfortable for you, I strongly advise you to work with a good counselor who advocates awareness.

This awareness piece is the key to combating destructive beliefs. You first have to notice *that* you're doing it before you can make any changes. The next time a lie comes into your thinking, catch it. Look at it. What is it saying about you? Challenge it. How is the thought supported? Where is it from? Now shift to what God says is true about you. Where does that statement come from? If God is who He says He is, can His statements be lies? There is no partiality with God. If He says you are a magnificent creation, He is speaking to all of His creation. That statement includes you no matter what you have done, said, or thought. No matter how any one's actions or words might have led you to believe otherwise, soak in the truth. Each time the lies enter into your thinking, be aware of them, stop them in their tracks, and immediately challenge them with the truth. This means you have the truth at your disposal, so begin learning the truths about yourself. Here are a bunch of them, but the Bible is full of how much God loves and cherishes you. *You are:*

- Made in God's image (Genesis 1:27)

- Not God! (Job 38-42)

- Known completely, never abandoned, created wonderfully and with intention (Psalm 139:1-16)

- Healed, set free, and comforted; beautiful, joyful, and a display of God's splendor (Isaiah 61:1-3)

- Not condemned; set free from everything you have done wrong –past, present, & future (Romans 8:1-2)

- Cheered on by God (Romans 8:31)

- Never separated from God. Nothing you, anyone or anything else does can remove God's love for you (Romans 8:38-39)

- Given the opportunity to live with a clear conscience, aware of your sin but not weighed down by it (I Corinthians 4:3-5; Hebrews 9:13-14)

- Chosen and part of His plan (Ephesians 1:11-12)

- Alive, raised up with Christ, saved through faith, God's workmanship, and created to do good works (Ephesians 2:1-10)

- Able to access the Father through Christ (Ephesians 2:18)

- A member of God's family (Ephesians 2:19)

- Completely forgiven (Colossians 2:13)

- Desired by Satan; by humbling yourself before God, He will lift you up and make you strong for His glory (I Peter 5:6-10)

- Stronger than the lies that will try to sway you from God's truth (I John 4:1-6)

- Able to rely on God's love because He is love (I John 4:16)

I tell my clients (and I do this myself) to write the truths about themselves on sticky notes and put them everywhere. You can put them on your dashboard, in your calendar, on your cell phone, on your bathroom mirror, on your refrigerator, on your computer, and on your TV. Take time to notice when you may be most susceptible to the lies, and make certain you have the truth nearby during those times. It's called being ready. You can try and try to challenge lies, but if you don't do the work of writing the truths down and learning them, you will have a harder time seeing a change. This requires work. Autopilot does not require work, which is why most of us slip into that mode. Just ask yourself if you really want to continue living this way and believing the lies about yourself. If the answer is yes, then continue on. If the answer is no, then it is up to you to make the change. God will help you if you ask Him, but He rarely does the work for you. Miracles do occur, but that is not the typical experience. It is just like deciding to run a marathon; you will never get across the finish line by sitting on the couch. Point made? *We need some help!*

Hebrews 10:35–36 says "Do not throw away your confidence it will be richly rewarded. You need to persevere so that when you have done the will of God, you will receive what he has promised." I so wish I could have experienced that in my first marriage and been able to persevere. I do not have the past; I have this moment—now. In my present and looking forward, I choose to persevere in the relationship I have with David, raising my kids, in my work, and even in writing this book. I want to persevere in each piece of my life God has given me. One thing I have learned from my affair is that I can *want* to make good choices, but on my own, I will more than likely stumble into a heaping mess of trouble! I have that ability mastered. As often as I remember, I relinquish the reins of my control to God's trustworthy hands. I know that while I am incapable of holding it all together and living out even my good wants, He can equip me to do more than I could ever imagine possible.

Take the writing of this book, for example. I think it's a decent idea, but I have fought with it since day one. That was five years ago! This book isn't that long and didn't require hours and hours of research, and still it was a labor of torture. I have the utmost respect for writers. This is the hardest project I have undertaken. I have noticed that the times when I force myself to slog through, thinking, "You will write this book. Now sit down and start typing those words!" I feel like I'm swimming through freshly poured cement. Water gets added to the cement when I say, "OK, Lord, I am asking You to write through me. I don't want this to be my book, but rather it is Yours."

Despite the challenges, I wanted to write this book. The initial idea came out of my desire to equip women with the tools necessary to avoid taking the road I spiraled down. I was thinking that if I had a book like this, it's possible I would have made different choices. I'm not certain that's true, but that was my initial thought. As I experienced more healing, I thought that I could shed some light on the deep need for acceptance of those who veer off the straight and narrow (is there anyone who hasn't?). When my motives were pure, writing came easier—not easy, just easier.

At times I noticed revenge creeping in. If I could write a successful book, then I would be reaccepted into my church community. That would show them. I'm really a great person, and you'll acknowledge it when you see my book. The problem with that kind of thinking is that it is all about me. It's about what *I* can do and how great you'll think *I* am. The truth is *I* had an affair. *I* tanked my marriage. *I* alienated people. *I* persecute my husband. *I* am self-seeking … I just humbly ask God nearly every day to take over. I say, "I'm stepping aside so You can shine, Lord." I even need His help in stepping aside. I'll tell you, this writing experience has been much more enjoyable with God at the helm.

We desperately need each other, too. We simply cannot change without the support of others. It's hard to find safe people. Start with groups in your church or perhaps a recovery group like Celebrate Recovery, Alcoholics Anonymous, AlAnon,

Codependents Anonymous, or Overeaters Anonymous. There are many to choose from. Start with one person, but don't stop there. Begin sharing bits of your story, slowly building trust with someone. Be a trustworthy and safe person in return. The benefits of connecting and revealing your truth are staggering—joy, a lighter load, healing, growth, and freedom!

You can even use this book as a way to break the silence. Form a group, read it together, and discuss it. Maybe, just maybe, you will start tearing down the walls that isolate us. You can bridge the gap and create pockets of people who are willing to be vulnerable and propelled toward healing.

Know that I am praying for you to turn back and strengthen others!

The following are websites where you can find more information on:

Karen and her counseling practice:
journeyforward.net

This book:
survivingthescarletletter.com

Henry Cloud and John Townsend as well as
the Ultimate Leadership Intensive and the
One Week Intensive for counselors:
cloudtownsend.com

EMDR:
EMDRIA.org

Shadow Work:
ShadowWork.com